RESISTENCIA

RESISTENCIA
POEMS OF PROTEST AND REVOLUTION

INTRODUCTION BY **JULIA ALVAREZ**

EDITED BY **MARK EISNER** & **TINA ESCAJA**

TIN HOUSE / Portland, Oregon

Published by Tin House, Portland, Oregon

Distributed by W. W. Norton & Company

Library of Congress Cataloging-in-Publication Data

Names: Alvarez, Julia, writer of introduction. | Eisner, Mark, 1973- editor. | Escaja, Tina, editor.
Title: Resistencia : poems of protest and revolution / introduction by Julia Alvarez ; edited by Mark Eisner & Tina Escaja.
Description: Portland, Oregon : Tin House, [2020] | Parallel text of original poems and English translations. Original languages include Spanish, French, Portuguese, Kaqchikel, Mapudungun, Miskito, and Quechua.
Identifiers: LCCN 2020015632 | ISBN 9781951142070 (paperback) | ISBN 9781951142087 (ebook)
Subjects: LCSH: Protest poetry, Latin American—Translations into English.
Classification: LCC PN6110.P83 R47 2020 | DDC 808.81/9998--dc23
LC record available at https://lccn.loc.gov/2020015632

First US Edition 2020
Printed in the USA
Interior design by Jakob Vala

www.tinhouse.com

DICEN LOS VIEJOS BARDOS

No lo olvides, poeta.
En cualquier sitio y época
en que hagas o en que sufras la Historia,
siempre estará acechándote algún poema peligroso.

—Heberto Padilla, Cuba

THE OLD BARDS SPEAK

Don't forget it, poet.
Whatever the place and time
in which you make or suffer History,
there will always be a dangerous poem waiting to ambush you.

—translated by Mark Strand

CONTENTS

REBEL WORDS

There is a strong and vibrant tradition in the Americas of a poetry of witness. This should come as no surprise in a hemisphere carved out of violence, wrested from the Indigenous, built on the backs of the enslaved, the conquered, the murdered, the raped. Often all that was left to the powerless was the power of testimony; the only rebellion possible was that of the rebel word, to quote the title of Raquel Verdesoto de Romo Dávila's poem included in this anthology. Even when nothing remained but walls erected to prohibit passage, to imprison and entomb, to serve as backdrops for firing squads, those walls became the printing presses of the poor. Scrawled on them were messages voicing resistance and giving hope. To this day the tradition persists. On one wall recently photographed at the border between Mexico and the United States, a message reads: *They tried to bury us. They did not know we were seeds.*

This anthology is evidence of the flowering of those seeds.

"The struggle of man against power is the struggle of memory against forgetting," the novelist Milan Kundera once wrote, and it is a struggle with deep roots in the southern reaches of this hemisphere, a struggle that continues to this day (turn on the news) and is powerfully audible in this anthology. "The South also exists . . . where memory / omits no memories," Mario Benedetti reminds the forgetful North in his wry poem "El Sur también existe." El Norte might consider such notions "magical realism," fanciful theories for academics to parse out—like Papa Hegel in René Depestre's poem, who understands

> the laws and secrets of humanity's
> great history, but he has no brother's
> eyes for the bleak veins running
> in panic in the wood of black woe.

But in the poems of these poets from el Sur, the dead, the forgotten, the voiceless and faceless rise up. Pablo Neruda refuses to bury his poetry's head in the nostalgic imagery "of dreams, of the leaves, / of the great volcanoes of his native land." He will not be silenced, whether the struggle is in his native Chile or with his brother poets in the Spanish Civil War. "Come and see the blood in streets, / come and see / the blood in the streets, / come and see the blood / in the streets!" he shouts at the end of "I Explain Some Things." As if answering that summons, Julia de Burgos rises up, "I felt myself a blossom of all the soils of the earth, / of the soils without history." Yes, the land, too, speaks (Óscar Cerruto's Altiplano, Ernest Pépin's Guadeloupe), along with mahogany trees and rushing rivers. Don't fool yourselves, Ernesto Cardenal warns, "Not only humans longed for liberation."

Memory is, in fact, the South's most powerful and plentiful resource. "The poor are many / and so / it's impossible to forget them," Roberto Sosa writes. Together they are a force that cannot be defeated.

They can
carry on their shoulders
the coffin of a star.

They can
destroy the air like furious birds,
to blot out the sun.

The danger comes when the poor are "unaware of their treasures." But the poems remind us.

The witness borne in these pages can sometimes feel overwhelming. On one read-through I marked the margins of the index with a tiny cross for every writer who had been murdered, tortured, exiled, or had succumbed to despair and suicide. The pages looked like a cemetery. But turn to the poems themselves, and the poets are resurrected, their voices defiant, alive, presente! Víctor Jara, arrested and corralled in a stadium with hundreds of other students and teachers, later shot forty-four times, his musician hands crushed, keeps on singing in his poem "Estadio Chile." In his moving documentary *Pablo Neruda! Presente!*, Mark Eisner, one of the editors of this anthology, recounts the story of the poet's funeral in Santiago. Unable to mount a demonstration because of the military takeover, mourners marched behind the coffin instead, ten thousand strong, shouting the phrase "Neruda, presente!" With each entry in *Resistencia*, the chorus grows: Vallejo, presente! Césaire, presente! Storni, presente! Dalton, presente! Vilariño, presente! On and on and on. It is a thrilling experience of solidarity to read these pages.

One of the strengths of this anthology is its radical inclusiveness. Editors Tina Escaja and Mark Eisner have assembled a diverse brigada Américana, armed with weapons of mass creation. Here the reader will encounter well-known poets (Neruda, Vallejo, Mistral, Césaire), as well as lesser-known ones—at least to this reader (Evaristo, Cuevas Cob, Galván, Chihuailaf). There are voices that have been traditionally excluded, even at times in leftist literary circles: the voices of women; Indigenous voices; the voices of those with different sexual orientations; voices from across Latin America as well as the Caribbean: poets writing not just in Spanish, but in French, Portuguese, Kreyòl, Quechua, Mapudungun. Humor and irony and sassiness abound: Reina María Rodríguez wrests the mythic apple from Eve and gives it instead to her daughter so that she won't be cowed, impoverished, kept in the dark—so that "she won't turn out like me"; José Leonel Rugama enumerates the mounting cost of space exploration in a seemingly simple and childlike counting poem, then juxtaposes this expense with the mounting hunger of the Acahualincan people, which has resulted in their extinction—but no matter: "Blessed are the poor for they shall inherit the moon"; Rei Berroa writes gleefully about the poetic justice of doves landing on the statues of tyrants and dictators, leaving behind a mantle of poop!

Ultimately, what comes through is not a graveyard of poems by victims or about victimhood, but a chorus of love and hope. This is important as we continue to face the forces that would drown out and negate this chorus: there is no stopping this river of voices, these currents of song. "Listen to me!" Miguel Otero Silva writes in "Sowing":

I aspire for us to live
in the vibrant voices of morning.

XX

> I want to remain together with you
> in the deep sap of humanity

To read through these poems is to be reminded again and again of our true allegiance to each other. That is where Bertalicia Peralta takes us in her astonishing poem "The Only Woman":

> the only woman, the only one that she can be
> is the one who, aching and clean, decides for herself
> to leave her prehistory behind.

Walking "tall and true," this new woman "unlearns the alphabet of submission" and "frees herself through the fullness of love." She leads us beyond resistance and struggle to what would indeed be a promised land, not located in any one country in the hemisphere, but in that "Altiplano sin fronteras," that high plain without borders, which is another name for love.

—Julia Alvarez
2019

RESISTENCIA

LITTLE FEET

for Doña Isaura Dinator

Children's little feet,
blue with cold,
how can they see you and not cover you
dear Lord!

Little feet battered
by every stone,
abused by snow
and mud!

Man, blind, does not see
that in your wake
you leave
a flower of living light;

that where you set
your small bleeding sole,
the tuberose blooms more
sweetly.

Be heroic as you walk
the straight paths,
for you are
perfect.

PIECECITOS

a doña Isaura Dinator

Piececitos de niño,
azulosos de frío,
¡cómo os ven y no os cubren,
Dios mío!

¡Piececitos heridos
por los guijarros todos,
ultrajados de nieves
y lodos!

El hombre ciego ignora
que por donde pasáis,
una flor de luz viva
dejáis;

que allí donde ponéis
la plantita sangrante,
el nardo nace más
fragante.

Sed, puesto que marcháis
por los caminos rectos,
heroicos como sois
perfectos.

Children's little feet,
two small suffering jewels,
how can people pass right by
and not see you!

translated by Jessica Powell

Editors' note: In the Spanish original, Mistral employs a specific rhyme scheme that makes the poem sound like a lullaby. Though it means the loss of some of this melodiousness, for the English translation we have decided not to maintain the rhyme scheme, as to do so would excessively distort the poem's original meaning. However, we do suggest you read the original to hear that melody, even if you don't understand Spanish well.

Piececitos de niño,
dos joyitas sufrientes,
¡cómo pasan sin veros
las gentes!

MASS

    At the end of the battle,
the combatant dead, a man approached him
and said to him: "Don't die, I love you so much!"
But the corpse, alas! kept on dying.

    Two more came up to him and repeated:
"Don't leave us! Be brave! Come back to life!"
But the corpse, alas! kept on dying.

    Twenty, a hundred, a thousand, five hundred thousand appeared,
crying out: "So much love, and no power against death!"
But the corpse, alas! kept on dying.

    Millions of individuals surrounded him,
with a common plea: "Don't leave us, brother!"
But the corpse, alas! kept on dying.

    Then, all the inhabitants of the earth
surrounded him; the corpse looked at them sadly, deeply moved;
he got up slowly,
embraced the first man; started to walk . . .

translated by Clayton Eshleman

MASA

Al fin de la batalla,
y muerto ya el combatiente, vino hacia él un hombre
y le dijo: "No mueras, te amo tanto!"
Pero el cadáver ¡ay! siguió muriendo.

Se le acercaron dos y repitiéronle:
"No nos dejes! ¡Valor! ¡Vuelve a la vida!"
Pero el cadáver ¡ay! siguió muriendo.

Acudieron a él veinte, cien, mil, quinientos mil,
clamando: "¡Tanto amor y no poder nada contra la muerte!"
Pero el cadáver ¡ay! siguió muriendo.

Le rodearon millones de individuos,
con un ruego común: "¡Quédate, hermano!"
Pero el cadáver ¡ay! siguió muriendo.

Entonces, todos los hombres de la tierra
le rodearon; les vió el cadáver triste, emocionado;
incorporóse lentamente,
abrazó al primer hombre; echóse a andar . . .

YOU WANT ME WHITE

You want me light,
Like sea-foam you want me,
like mother-of-pearl.
That I be a lily
Chaste, above all lilies.
A delicate perfume.
Closed corolla.

No moonbeam
Has passed through me.
No daisy
Calls herself my sister.
You want me snow,
You want me white,
You want me dawn.

You who had all
The cups at hand,
Lips purple
From honey and fruit.
You who at the banquet
Covered with vines
Abandoned your flesh
Celebrating Bacchus.
You who in the black

TÚ ME QUIERES BLANCA

Tú me quieres alba,
Me quieres de espumas,
Me quieres de nácar.
Que sea azucena
Sobre todas, casta.
De perfume tenue.
Corola cerrada.

Ni un rayo de luna
Filtrado me haya.
Ni una margarita
Se diga mi hermana.
Tú me quieres nívea,
Tú me quieres blanca,
Tú me quieres alba.

Tú que hubiste todas
Las copas a mano,
De frutos y mieles
Los labios morados.
Tú que en el banquete
Cubierto de pámpanos
Dejaste las carnes
Festejando a Baco.
Tú que en los jardines

Gardens of Deceit
Dressed in red
Spread Havoc.

You whose skeleton
Remains intact
By what miracles
I still don't know,
You desire me white
(God forgive you),
You desire me chaste
(God forgive you),
You desire me dawn!

Flee to the forest;
Go to the mountains;
Cleanse your mouth;
Live in a hut;
Touch with your hands
The damp earth;
Feed your body
With bitter roots;
Drink from the rocks;
Sleep on frost;
Renew your tissues
With saltpeter and water;
Speak with the birds
And arise at dawn.

Negros del Engaño
Vestido de rojo
Corriste al Estrago.

Tú que el esqueleto
Conservas intacto
No sé todavía
Por cuáles milagros,
Me pretendes blanca
(Dios te lo perdone),
Me pretendes casta
(Dios te lo perdone),
¡Me pretendes alba!

Huye hacia los bosques;
Vete a la montaña;
Límpiate la boca;
Vive en las cabañas;
Toca con las manos
La tierra mojada;
Alimenta el cuerpo
Con raíz amarga;
Bebe de las rocas;
Duerme sobre escarcha;
Renueva tejidos
Con salitre y agua;
Habla con los pájaros
Y lévate al alba.

And when your flesh
Has been transformed,
And when into it
You've put your soul
Which in bedrooms
Remained entangled,
Then, good man,
Ask me to be white,
Ask me to be snow,
Ask me to be chaste.

translated by Barbara Paschke

Y cuando las carnes
Te sean tornadas,
Y cuando hayas puesto
En ellas el alma
Que por las alcobas
Se quedó enredada,
Entonces, buen hombre,
Preténdeme blanca,
Preténdeme nívea,
Preténdeme casta.

INTERNATIONAL SYMPOSIUM ON FEAR

For the time being we won't sing of love,
which has fled beyond all undergrounds.
We'll sing of fear, which sterilizes all hugs.
We won't sing of hatred, since it doesn't exist,
only fear exists, our father and our companion,
the dread fear of hinterlands, oceans, deserts,
the fear of soldiers, fear of mothers, fear of churches,
we'll sing of the fear of dictators, of democrats,
we'll sing of the fear of death and what's after death,
then we'll die of fear,
and fearful yellow flowers will sprout on our tombs.

translated by Richard Zenith

CONGRESSO INTERNACIONAL DO MEDO

Provisoriamente não cantaremos o amor,
que se refugiou mais abaixo dos subterrâneos.
Cantaremos o medo, que esteriliza os abraços,
não cantaremos o ódio, porque este não existe,
existe apenas o medo, nosso pai e nosso companheiro,
o medo grande dos sertões, dos mares, dos desertos,
o medo dos soldados, o medo das mães, o medo das igrejas,
cantaremos o medo dos ditadores, o medo dos democratas,
cantaremos o medo da morte e o medo de depois da morte.
Depois morreremos de medo
e sobre nossos túmulos nascerão flores amarelas e medrosas.

SENSEMAYÁ (SONG FOR THE KILLING OF A SNAKE)

¡Mayombe—bombe—mayombé!
¡Mayombe—bombe—mayombé!
¡Mayombe—bombe—mayombé!

Snake has eyes of glass;
snake comes and coils on a branch;
with its eyes of glass, on a branch,
with its eyes of glass.
Snake walks down without feet;
snake hides in the green;
walking it hides in the green,
walking without feet.

¡Mayombe—bombe—mayombé!
¡Mayombe—bombe—mayombé!
¡Mayombe—bombe—mayombé!

Strike it with the hatchet, and it dies:
strike it now!
Don't strike it with your foot, it will bite you,
don't strike it with your foot, it will escape!

SENSEMAYÁ (CANTO PARA MATAR A UNA CULEBRA)

¡Mayombe—bombe—mayombé!
¡Mayombe—bombe—mayombé!
¡Mayombe—bombe—mayombé!

La culebra tiene los ojos de vidrio;
la culebra viene y se enreda en un palo;
con sus ojos de vidrio, en un palo,
con sus ojos de vidrio.
La culebra camina sin patas;
la culebra se esconde en la yerba;
caminando se esconde en la yerba,
caminando sin patas.

¡Mayombe—bombe—mayombé!
¡Mayombe—bombe—mayombé!
¡Mayombe—bombe—mayombé!

Tú le das con el hacha, y se muere:
¡dale ya!
¡No le des con el pie, que te muerde,
no le des con el pie, que se va!

Sensemayá, the snake,
sensemayá.
Sensemayá, with its eyes,
sensemayá.
Sensemayá, with its tongue,
sensemayá.
Sensemayá, with its mouth,
sensemayá . . .

Dead snake cannot feed;
dead snake cannot whistle;
it cannot walk,
it cannot flee!
The dead snake cannot see;
the dead snake cannot swallow;
cannot breathe,
cannot fang!

¡Mayombe—bombe—mayombé!
Sensemayá, the snake . . .
¡Mayombe—bombe—mayombé!
Sensemayá, does not slither . . .
¡Mayombe—bombe—mayombé!
Sensemayá, the snake . . .
¡Mayombe—bombe—mayombé!
Sensemayá, dead now!

translated by Juan Felipe Herrera

Sensemayá, la culebra,
sensemayá.
Sensemayá, con sus ojos,
sensemayá.
Sensemayá, con su lengua,
sensemayá.
Sensemayá, con su boca,
sensemayá . . .

¡La culebra muerta no puede comer;
la culebra muerta no puede silbar;
no puede caminar,
no puede correr!
¡La culebra muerta no puede mirar;
la culebra muerta no puede beber;
no puede respirar,
no puede morder!

¡Mayombe—bombe—mayombé!
Sensemayá, la culebra . . .
¡Mayombe—bombe—mayombé!
Sensemayá, no se mueve . . .
¡Mayombe—bombe—mayombé!
Sensemayá, la culebra . . .
¡Mayombe—bombe—mayombé!
Sensemayá, se murió!

I EXPLAIN SOME THINGS

You will ask: And where are the lilacs?
And the metaphysics laced with poppies?
And the rain that often beat
his words filling them
with holes and birds?

I'll tell you everything that's happening with me.

I lived in a neighborhood
of Madrid, with church bells,
with clocks, with trees.

From there you could see
the dry face of Castilla
like an ocean of leather.
                My house was called
the house of flowers, because everywhere
geraniums were exploding: it was
a beautiful house
with dogs and little kids.
                Raúl, do you remember?
Do you remember, Rafael?
                Federico, you remember,
from under the earth,
do you remember my house with balconies on which

EXPLICO ALGUNAS COSAS

Preguntaréis: Y dónde están las lilas?
Y la metafísica cubierta de amapolas?
Y la lluvia que a menudo golpeaba
sus palabras llenándolas
de agujeros y pájaros?

Os voy a contar todo lo que me pasa.

Yo vivía en un barrio
de Madrid, con campanas,
con relojes, con árboles.

Desde allí se veía
el rostro seco de Castilla
como un océano de cuero.
                    Mi casa era llamada
la casa de las flores, porque por todas partes
estallaban geranios: era
una bella casa
con perros y chiquillos.
                    Raúl, te acuerdas?
Te acuerdas, Rafael?
                    Federico, te acuerdas
debajo de la tierra,
te acuerda de mi casa con balcones en donde

the light of June drowned flowers in your mouth?

                                                 Hermano, hermano!

Everything
was great voices, salty goods,
piles of throbbing bread,
markets of my Argüelles neighborhood with its statue
like a pale inkwell among the carp:
oil flowed into the spoons,
a loud pulse
of feet and hands filled the streets,
meters, liters, sharp
essence of life,
                  piled fish,
texture of rooftops under a cold sun that
wears out the weather vane,
fine delirious ivory of the potatoes,
tomatoes repeating all the way to the sea.

And one morning everything was burning
and one morning the fires
were shooting out of the earth
devouring beings,
and ever since then fire,
gunpowder ever since,
and ever since then blood.
Bandits with airplanes and with Moors,
bandits with finger rings and duchesses,
bandits with black friars making blessings,

la luz de junio ahogaba flores en tu boca?

Hermano, hermano!

Todo
eran grandes voces; sal de mercaderías,
aglomeraciones de pan palpitante,
mercados de mi barrio de Argüelles con su estatua
como un tintero pálido entre las merluzas:
el aceite llegaba a las cucharas,
un profundo latido
de pies y manos llenaba las calles,
metros, litros, esencia
aguda de la vida,

                pescados hacinados,
contextura de techos con sol frío en el cual
la flecha se fatiga,
delirante marfil fino de las patatas,
tomates repetidos hasta el mar.

Y una mañana todo estaba ardiendo
y una mañana las hogueras
salían de la tierra
devorando seres,
y desde entonces fuego,
pólvora desde entonces,
y desde entonces sangre.
Bandidos con aviones y con moros,
bandidos con sortijas y duquesas,
banditos con frailes negros bendiciendo

kept coming from the sky to kill children,
and through the streets the blood of the children
ran simply, like children's blood.

Jackals the jackal would reject,
stones the dry thistle would bite then spit out,
vipers the vipers would despise!

Facing you I have seen the blood
of Spain rise up
to drown you in one single wave
of pride and knives!

Traitor
generals:
behold my dead house,
behold Spain destroyed:
yet instead of flowers from every dead house
burning metal flows,
yet from every hollow of Spain
Spain flows,
yet from every dead child rises a rifle with eyes,
yet from every crime bullets are born
that one day will find the target
of your heart.

You will ask why his poetry
doesn't speak to us of dreams, of the leaves,
of the great volcanoes of his native land?

venían por el cielo a matar niños,
y por las calles la sangre de los niños
corría simplemente, como sangre de niños.

Chacales que el chacal rechazaría,
piedras que el cardo seco mordería escupiendo,
víboras que las víboras odiaran!

Frente a vosotros he visto la sangre
de España levantarse
para ahogaros en una sola ola
de orgullo y de cuchillos!

Generales
traidores:
mirad mi casa muerta,
mirad España rota:
pero de cada casa muerta sale metal ardiendo
en vez de flores,
pero de cada hueco de España
sale España,
pero de cada niño muerto sale un fusil con ojos,
pero de cada crimen nacen balas
que os hallarán un día el sitio
del corazón.

Preguntaréis por qué su poesía
no nos habla del sueño, de las hojas,
de los grandes volcanes de su país natal?

Come and see the blood in the streets,
come and see
the blood in the streets,
come and see the blood
in the streets!

translated by Mark Eisner

Venid a ver la sangre por las calles,
venid a ver
la sangre por las calles,
venid a ver la sangre
por las calles!

SOWING

When all that's left of me is a tree,
when my bones have scattered
under mother earth;
when nothing's left of you but a white rose
watered with what you once were
and the breath of the kiss which we drink today
has set sail in a thousand different breezes;
when our names
are sounded without echo
slumbering in the shade of a soundless oblivion;
you will go on living in the beauty of the rose,
as I shall, in the leaves of the tree
and our love, in the murmur of the wind.

Listen to me!
I aspire for us to live
in the vibrant voices of morning.

I want to remain together with you
in the deep sap of humanity:
in the laughter of children,
in the peace of humankind,
in a love without tears.

SIEMBRA

Cuando de mí no quede sino un árbol,
cuando mis huesos se hayan esparcido
bajo la tierra madre;
cuando de ti no quede sino una rosa blanca
que se nutrió de aquello que tú fuiste
y haya zarpado ya con mil brisas distintas
el aliento del beso que hoy bebemos;
cuando ya nuestros nombres
sean sonidos sin eco
dormidos en la sombra de un olvido insondable;
tú seguirás viviendo en la belleza de la rosa,
como yo en el follaje del árbol
y nuestro amor en el murmullo de la brisa.

¡Escúchame!
Yo aspiro a que vivamos
en las vibrantes voces de la mañana.

Yo quiero perdurar junto contigo
en la savia profunda de la humanidad:
en la risa del niño,
en la paz de los hombres,
en el amor sin lagrimas.

That is why,
as we must give ourselves to the rose and to the tree,
to the earth and to the wind,
I beg of you that we give ourselves to the future of this world . . .

translated by Emily Toder

Por eso,
como habremos de darnos a la rosa y al árbol,
a la tierra y al viento,
te pido que nos demos al futuro del mundo . . .

THE REBEL WORD

We must hate that kind of peace
where men sowed winter
the shimmering of a four-leaf clover
that only unfolds inside fenced lands.
If clouds gallop by
let them give us water as they come near
if there is bread, in pieces
if a book adorns our hands
let reading voices roar.

translated by Juan Felipe Herrera

LA PALABRA REBELDE

Hay que odiar esa paz
donde los hombres sembraron el invierno
la hermosura del trébol
que se abre solamente en los campos cercados.
Si galopan las nubes
que se acerquen a todos a dar agua
si hay pan, en pedazos
si un libro nos adorna las manos
que lean altavoces.

GUAYASAMÍN, YOU!

Your force, Guayasamín, from what realm does it rise?
Castigating dove, hollering blood.
What eons formed your eyes that pierce worlds unseen,
your hands that ignite the heavens?
Listen, brother who burns
the suffering days
the days that wound
the night that makes for tears,
a man man-eater
onto eternity fixed by you
in such a manner no one will decipher how to unlock him
you hurled him we do not know across what perimeters.

Let that man shed tears
may he absorb the silk breath of the dove
may he be nourished on the power of the winds,
in your name.
Wayasamín is your name;
the rumble of the last solar sons
the freeze-chatter of the sacred eagles that wing-ruffle Quito
the howls that sharpened the eternal snowfall
and shadow-thickened the heavens even more.
Add this:
the suffering of the peoples of all the pueblos;
United States, China, Tawantinsuyo

IMAN GUAYASAMIN

¿Maypachamantan Guayasamin kallpayki oqarikun?
Qaqchaq urpi, yawar qapariq
¿maypachamantapunin ukupacha kanchariq ñawiki
cielo kañaq makiyki?
Uyuriway, rauraq wayqey.
Ñakay pacha mitata
runa kiriq punchauta,
waqachiq tuta
runa, runa mikuq uyanta,
wiña wiñaypaq churanki
mana pipa kuyuchiy atinanta
¡maykamaraq changanki!

Runa wagacun
wayrapa kallpanta mikuchun,
qan rayku.
Wayasamin sutiyki
intipa quepa ñeqen churinkunapa qaparisganmi
Quito muyup apu wamanikunapa katatatasqan
waqascan, riti mirasqan,
cielomantapas astawan sinchi sombran.
Manan chayllachu:
Estados Unidos, China, Tawantinsuyu
tukuy llaqtapi runakuna ñakasqanta,
imaymana mañakusqanmanta

everything they wish to reclaim and nurture.
You, brother who burns
shall shout all of this
with a voice more colossal
and rebellious than the Apurímac.
Very well hermano,
very well, Oswaldo.

translated by Juan Felipe Herrera

Editors' note: The poet's widow, Sybila Arredondo de Arguedas, in-
formed us that this poem, an homage to the Ecuadorian artist Oswaldo
Guayasamín, was originally written in Quechua. José María had not
finished translating it into Spanish by the time of his suicide. It was
completed later by Jesús Ruiz Durand. The English translation is based
on the completed Spanish.

qan, rauraq waygey, qaparinki,
Apurimaq mayu astawan hatun
astawan mana tanichiq simiwan.
¡Allinmi, waygey! ¡Estabín, Oswaldo!

SO MANY TIMES

So many times I'm frightened by my consciousness of race
and like a dog at night
baying at some
impending death
I always feel ready to foam with rage
against the things around me
against the things that kept me
forever from being
a man

And nothing
nothing would quell my hatred quite so much
as a pretty pool
of blood
made
with those sharp broad blades
that strip to the skin
our rum-rich hills

translated by Norman Shapiro

SI SOUVENT

Si souvent mon sentiment de race m'effraie
autant qu'un chien aboyant la nuit
une mort prochaine
quelconque
je me sens prêt à écumer toujours de rage
contre ce qui m'entoure
contre ce qui m'empêche
à jamais d'être
un homme

Et rien
rien ne saurait autant calmer ma haine
qu'une belle mare
de sang
faite
de ces coutelas tranchants
qui mettent à nu
les mornes à rhum

THE HIGH PLAIN

1

The high plain is immeasurable as a memory.
Skin of armadillo, it touches with its borders the four corners
    of the sky,
blows its dense, beastly breeze.
    The high plain shines like steel.
Its lunar solitude, rebellion drum,
thrashing of legends.
Women shepherds of torrents and sorrows,
the virgins of the earth, feed the fire of music.
Men, in the metal of their hair,
take in the hot scent of combat.
High plain creased by journeys and by pain
like a miner's palm.

ALTIPLANO

1

El Altiplano es inmensurable como un recuerdo.
Piel de kirquincho, toca con sus extremos las cuatro puntas
    del cielo,
sopla su densa brisa de bestia.
El Altiplano es resplandeciente como un acero.
Su soledad de luna, tambor de las sublevaciones,
solfatara de las leyendas.
Pastoras de turbiones y pesares,
las vírgenes de la tierra alimentan la hoguera de la música.
Los hombres, en el metal de sus cabellos,
asilan el caliente perfume de los combates.
Altiplano rayado de caminos y de tristeza
como palma del minero.

2

The high plain is as common as hate.
It blinds, suddenly, like a surge of blood.
High plain hard with ice
and where the cold is blue as the skin of the dead.
On its loins tattooed by the rough needles of time
the Aymaran laborers, their own tombs on their backs,
drive off with their rifles and slingshots the birds of the night.
Their lives, marked up, cut out, by the silence of the fire pits
while their bones are flooded by the rain and the song of the
    goldfinch.

3

High plain without borders,
laid open and violent as fire.

Its charangos accentuate the color of misfortune.
Its pierced solitude, drop by drop, the stone.

translated by Emily Toder and Mark Eisner

2

El Altiplano es frecuente como el odio.
Ciega, de pronto, como una oleada de sangre.
El Altiplano duro de hielos
y donde el frío es azul como la piel de los muertos.
Sobre su lomo tatuado por las agujas ásperas del tiempo
los labradores aymaras, su propia tumba a cuestas,
con los fusiles y la honda le ahuyentan pájaros de luz a la noche.
La vida se les tiza de silencio en los fogones
mientras las lluvias inundan sus huesos y el canto del
    jilguero.

3

Altiplano sin fronteras,
desplegado y violento como el fuego.

Sus charangos acentúan el color del infortunio.
Su soledad horada, gota a gota, la piedra.

PATIENCE OF SIGNS

sublime excoriations of a flesh fraternal and whipped to the
    point of rebellious fires in a thousand villages
arenas
fire
hulls' prophetic masts
fire
breeding ground for moray eels
fire riding lights of an island truly in distress
fires frantic tracks of haggard herds which in the mud are spelled
pieces of raw flesh
suspended spittings
a sponge dripping sour wine
a fiery waltz of lawns strewn with the cornets that fall from
    the broken surge of great tabebuias
fires shards lost in a desert of fears and cisterns
bones
dried-up fires never too dry for a worm to beat there tolling
    its new flesh
blue seeds of fire
fire of fires
witnesses of eyes which crazed for vengeance exhume
    themselves and expand
pollen pollen

PATIENCE DES SIGNES

sublimes excoriations d'une chair fraternelle et jusqu'aux feux
    rebelles de mille villages fouettée
arènes
feu
mât prophétique des carènes
feu
vivier des murènes feu
feu feux de position d'une île bien en peine
feux empreintes effrénées de hagards troupeaux qui dans les
    boues s'épellent
morceaux de chair crue
crachats suspendus
éponge dégouttant de fiel
valse de feu des pelouses jonchées des cornets qui tombent de
    l'élan brisé des grands tabebuias
feux tessons perdus en un désert de peurs et de citernes
os
feux desséchés jamais si desséchés que n'y batte un ver
sonnant sa chair neuve semences bleues du feu
feu des feux
témoins d'yeux qui pour les folles vengeances s'exhument et
    s'agrandissent
pollen pollen

and along the sands where the nocturnal berries of sweet
    manchineels swell
rich oranges always accessible to the sincerity of long long
    thirsts

translated by Clayton Eshleman and Annette Smith

et par les grèves où s'arrondissent les baies nocturnes des
   doux mancenilliers
bonnes oranges toujours accessibles à la sincérité des soifs
   longues

I WAS MY OWN ROUTE

I wanted to be like men wanted me to be:
an attempt at life;
a game of hide-and-seek with my being.
But I was made of nows,
and my feet level upon the promissory earth
would not accept walking backwards,
and went forward, forward,
mocking the ashes to reach the kiss
of the new paths.

At each advancing step on my route forward
my back was ripped by the desperate flapping wings
of the old guard.

But the branch was unpinned forever,
and at each new whiplash my look
separated more and more and more from the distant
familiar horizons;
and my face took the expression that came from within
the defined expression that hinted at a feeling
of intimate liberation;
a feeling dial surged
from the balance between my life
and the truth of the kiss of the new paths.

YO MISMA FUI MI RUTA

Yo quise ser como los hombres quisieron que yo fuese:
un intento de vida;
un juego al escondite con mi ser.
Pero yo estaba hecha de presentes,
y mis pies planos sobre la tierra promisora
no resistían caminar hacia atrás,
y seguían adelante, adelante,
burlando las cenizas para alcanzar el beso
de los senderos nuevos.

A cada paso adelantado en mi ruta hacia el frente
rasgaba mis espaldas el aleteo desesperado
de los troncos viejos.

Pero la rama estaba desprendida para siempre,
y a cada nuevo azote la mirada mía
se separaba más y más y más de los lejanos
horizontes aprendidos:
y mi rostro iba tomando la expresión que le venía de adentro,
la expresión definida que asomaba un sentimiento
de liberación íntima;
un sentimiento que surgía
del equilibrio sostenido entre mi vida
y la verdad del beso de los senderos nuevos.

Already my course now set in the present,
I felt myself a blossom of all the soils of the earth,
of the soils without history,
of the soils without a future,
of the soil always soil without edges
of all the men and all the epochs.

And I was all in me as was life in me . . .

I wanted to be like men wanted me to be:
an attempt at life;
a game of hide-and-seek with my being.
But I was made of nows;
when the heralds announced me
at the regal parade of the old guard,
the desire to follow men warped in me,
and the homage was left waiting for me.

translated by Jack Agüeros

Ya definido mi rumbo en el presente,
me sentí brote de todos los suelos de la tierra,
de los suelos sin historia,
de los suelos sin porvenir,
del suelo siempre suelo sin orillas
de todos los hombres y de todas las épocas.

Y fui toda en mí como fue en mí la vida . . .

Yo quise ser como los hombres quisieron que yo fuese:
un intento de vida;
un juego al escondite con mi ser.
Pero yo estaba hecha de presentes;
cuando ya los heraldos me anunciaban
en el regio desfile de los troncos viejos,
se me torció el deseo de seguir a los hombres,
y el homenaje se quedó esperándome.

THE SOUTH ALSO EXISTS

With its ritual of steel
its conspicuous chimneys
its clandestine wise men
its siren song
its neon skies
its Christmas sales
its cult of the heavenly father
and of epaulets
      with the keys to the kingdom
      it is the North that commands

but way down here
the hunger at hand
resorts to the bitter fruit
of what others decide
while time passes
and the parades pass
and they do other things
that the North doesn't ban
      with its hard hope
      the South also exists

EL SUR TAMBIÉN EXISTE

Con su ritual de acero
sus grandes chimeneas
sus sabios clandestinos
su canto de sirenas
sus cielos de neón
sus ventas navideñas
su culto de dios padre
y de las charreteras
          con sus llaves del reino
          el norte es el que ordena

pero aquí abajo abajo
el hambre disponible
recurre al fruto amargo
de lo que otros deciden
mientras el tiempo pasa
y pasan los desfiles
y se hacen otras cosas
que el norte no prohibe
          con su esperanza dura
          el sur también existe

with its preachers
with its poison gasses
its chicago school
its landowners

with its luxurious washcloths
and its poor bones
its spent defenses
its defense expenses
      with its feat of invasion
      it is the North that commands

but way down here
each one in their hiding place
there are men and women
who know what to hold on to
making the most of the sun
and the eclipses too
moving the useless aside
and using what is useful
      with its veteran faith
      the South also exists

con sus predicadores
sus gases que envenenan
su escuela de chicago
sus dueños de la tierra

con sus trapos de lujo
y su pobre osamenta
sus defensas gastadas
sus gastos de defensa
      con su gesta invasora
      el norte es el que ordena

pero aquí abajo abajo
cada uno en su escondite
hay hombres y mujeres
que saben a qué asirse
aprovechando el sol
y también los eclipses
apartando lo inútil
y usando lo que sirve
      con su fe veterana
      el sur también existe

with its French horn
and its Swedish academy
its American sauce
and its English wrenches
with all its missiles
and its encyclopedias
its intergalactic war
and its opulent brutality
            with all its laurels
            it is the North that commands

but way down here
close to the roots
is where memory
omits no memories

and there are those who are ready to resurrect themselves
and there are those who are ready to go out of their way
and so together they achieve
what was an impossibility
            that the whole world might know
            that the South also exists

translated by Mark Eisner

con su corno francés
y su academia sueca
su salsa americana
y sus llaves inglesas
con todos sus misiles
y sus enciclopedias
su guerra de galaxias
y su saña opulenta
     con todos sus laureles
     el norte es el que ordena

pero aquí abajo abajo
cerca de las raíces
es donde la memoria
ningún recuerdo omite

y hay quienes se desmueren
y hay quienes se desviven
y así entre todos logran
lo que era un imposible
     que todo el mundo sepa
     que el sur también existe

JUST TO SAY IT

What children of a good-for-nothing
what beasts
how else to say it
how
what accusatory finger is enough
what anathema
what cry
what word that is not an insult
would work
not to move them
or sway them
or stop them.
Just to say it.

translated by Emily Toder

SÓLO PARA DECIRLO

Qué hijos de una tal por cual
qué bestias
cómo decirlo de otro modo
cómo
qué dedo acusador es suficiente
qué anatema
qué llanto
qué palabra que no sea un insulto
serviría
no para conmoverlos
ni para convencerlos
ni para detenerlos.
Sólo para decirlo.

SILENCE NEAR AN ANCIENT STONE

Here I sit, with all my words untouched
like a basket of unripe fruit.
The fragments
of a thousand ancient toppled gods
seek themselves in my blood, bind themselves, wishing to
regain their stature.
From their destroyed mouths
a song tries to rise to my own mouth,
the smell of burned resins, some visage
in a mysterious carved rock.
But I am oblivion, betrayal,
the shell that didn't retain from the sea
even the echo of the smallest wave.
I do not look at the submerged temples;
I look only at the trees that move their vast shadows
atop the ruins, bite the passing wind
with their acid teeth.
And the symbols close up beneath my eyes like
a flower beneath a blind man's clumsy fingers.
But I know: behind
my body another body crouches,
and all around me many breaths
cross paths furtively
like nocturnal jungle animals.
I know, somewhere,

SILENCIO CERCA DE UNA PIEDRA ANTIGUA

Estoy aquí, sentada, con todas mis palabras
como con una cesta de fruta verde, intactas.
Los fragmentos
de mil dioses antiguos derribados
se buscan por mi sangre, se aprisionan, queriendo
recomponer su estatua.
De las bocas destruidas
quiere subir hasta mi boca un canto,
un olor de resinas quemadas, algún gesto
de misteriosa roca trabajada.
Pero soy el olvido, la traición,
el caracol que no guardó del mar
ni el eco de la más pequeña ola.
Y no miro los templos sumergidos;
sólo miro los árboles que encima de las ruinas
mueven su vasta sombra, muerden con dientes ácidos
el viento cuando pasa.
Y los signos se cierran bajo mis ojos como
la flor bajo los dedos torpísimos de un ciego.
Pero yo sé: detrás
de mi cuerpo otro cuerpo se agazapa,
y alrededor de mí muchas respiraciones
cruzan furtivamente
como los animales nocturnos en la selva.
Yo sé, en algún lugar,

just like
the cactus in the desert,
a starry heart of thorns
awaits a man as the cactus awaits rain.
But I don't know more than a few words
of the language on the stone
under which they buried my ancestor alive.

translated by Jessica Powell

lo mismo
que en el desierto el cactus,
un constelado corazón de espinas
está aguardando un hombre como el cactus la lluvia.
Pero yo no conozco más que ciertas palabras
en el idioma o lápida
bajo el que sepultaron vivo a mi antepasado.

LATIN AMERICA

My man
My back-up
My brother

Field-worker-to-my-side
Comrade
In-this-together

My friend
My boy
Paisano . . .

Here are my neighbors.
Here are my brothers.

Latin American the same faces
from any spot in América Latina:

Indoblackwhite
Blacknwhite
And blackindowhite

Thick-lipped blondes
Goateed Indians
And straight-haired blacks

AMÉRICA LATINA

Mi cuate
Mi socio
Mi hermano

Aparcero
Camarado
Compañero

Mi pata
M´hijito
Paisano . . .

He aquí mis vecinos.
He aquí mis hermanos.

Las mismas caras latinoamericanas
de cualquier punto de América Latina:

Indoblanquinegros
Blanquinegrindios
Y negrindoblancos

Rubias bembonas
Indios barbudos
Y negros lacios

Everyone complains
—Ah, if only in my country
there weren't so much politics!
—Ah, if only in my country
there weren't any paleolithics!
—Ah, if only in my country
there weren't militarism
nor oligarchy
nor chauvinism
nor bureaucracy
nor hypocrisy
nor clergy
nor anthropophagy . . .
—Ah, if only in my country . . .

Someone asks me where am I from
(I do not say the following):

I was born near Cuzco
I admire Puebla
I am inspired by Antillean rum
I sing with an Argentinian timbre
I pray to Santa Rosa de Lima
and the orishás de Bahía.

Todos se quejan:
—¡Ah, si en mi país
no hubiese tanta política. . . !
—¡Ah, si en mi país
no hubiera gente paleolítica. . . !
—¡Ah, si en mi país
no hubiese militarismo,
ni oligarquía
ni chauvinismo
ni burocracia
ni hipocresía
ni clerecía
ni antropofagia . . .
—¡Ah, si en mi país . . .

Alguien pregunta de dónde soy
(Yo no respondo lo siguiente):

Nací cerca del Cuzco
admiro a Puebla
me inspira el ron de las Antillas
canto con voz argentina
creo en Santa Rosa de Lima
y en los orishás de Bahía.

I did not color in my Continent
nor did I paint Brazil green
yellow Perú
red Bolivia.

I did not trace territorial lines
separating brother from sister.

I rest my forehead on the Río Grande
I attach as impervious stone to Cabo de Hornos
drown my left arm in the Pacific
submerge my right in the Atlantic.

Across coasts of east and west
two hundred miles I step into each ocean
one hand goes deep another hand
this is how I insist on our Continent
a Latin American embrace.

translated by Juan Felipe Herrera

Yo no coloreé mi Continente
ni pinté verde a Brasil
amarillo Perú
roja Bolivia.

Yo no tracé líneas territoriales
separando al hermano del hermano.

Poso la frente sobre Río Grande
me afirmo pétreo sobre el Cabo de Hornos
hundo mi brazo izquierdo en el Pacífico
y sumerjo mi diestra en el Atlántico.

Por las costas de oriente y occidente
doscientas millas entro a cada Océano
sumerjo mano y mano
y así me aferro a nuestro Continente
en un abrazo Latinoamericano.

ECOLOGY

You saw more coyotes near San Ubaldo in September.
And more alligators, a little after the triumph,
    in the rivers, there near San Ubaldo.
               More rabbits and raccoons on the road . . .
The bird population has tripled, they say,
    especially the *piches*.
The noisy *piches* go swim wherever they see the water shining.
The Somocistas destroyed the lakes, rivers, and mountains too.
    They diverted the course of the rivers for their farms.
The Ochomogo had dried up last summer.
The Sinecapa dried up because the landowners stripped the land.
The Río Grande of Matagalpa dried up during the war,
        there near the Sebaco Plains.
They built two dams on the Ochomogo,
             And the capitalist chemical wastes
spilled into the Ochomogo and the fish reeled around like drunks.
    The Boaco River carried sewage.
The Moyua Lagoon dried up. A Somocista colonel
robbed the peasants' land and built a dam.
The Moyua Lagoon that for centuries had been beautiful in that spot.
    (But the little fish will soon return.)
They stripped the land and built dams.
        Few *garrobos* in the sun, few armadillos.
Somoza sold the Caribbean green tortoise.
They exported *paslama* and iguana eggs by the truckload.

ECOLOGÍA

En septiembre por San Ubaldo se vieron más coyotes.
Más cuajipales, a poco del triunfo,
    en los ríos, allá por San Ubaldo.
        En la carretera más conejos, culumucos . . .
La población de pájaros se ha triplicado, nos dicen,
    en especial la de los piches.
Los bulliciosos piches bajan a nadar adonde ven el agua brillar.
Los somocistas también destruían los lagos, ríos, y montañas.
    Desviaban el curso de los ríos para sus fincas.
El Ochomogo se había secado el verano pasado.
El Sinecapa secado por el despale de los latifundistas.
El Río Grande de Matagalpa, secado, durante la guerra,
    allá por los llanos de Sébaco.
Dos represas pusieron al Ochomogo,
       y los desechos químicos capitalistas
caían en el Ochomogo y los pescados andaban como borrachos.
    El río de Boaco con aguas negras.
La laguna de Moyuá se había secado. Un coronel somocista
robó las tierras de los campesinos, y construyó una represa.
La laguna de Moyuá que por siglos estuvo bella en ese sitio.
    (Pero ya volverán los pescaditos.)
Despalaron y represaron.
      Pocos garrobos al sol, pocos cusucos.
La tortuga verde del Caribe la vendía Somoza.
En camiones exportaban los huevos de paslama y las iguanas.

The caguama tortoise finished.
The Gran Lago swordfish finished off by José Somoza.
Facing danger of extinction the jungle jaguar,
     its soft skin the color of the jungle,
and the puma, the tapir in the mountains
               (like the peasants in the mountains).
And the poor Chiquito River! Its misfortune
that of the whole country. Somocismo reflected in its waters.
The Chiquito River of León, fed by brooks
of sewage, soap factory and tannery wastes,
white water from the soap factories, red from the tanneries;
plastics, chamber pots, rusty iron in the riverbed. This
is what Somocismo left us.
(We have to see the river pretty and clear once again singing
     its way to the sea).
And into Lake Managua all of Managua's wastewaters
and chemical wastes.

          And there near Solentiname, on La Zanata Island:
a great white stinking heap of swordfish skeletons.
But the swordfish and freshwater sharks are breathing again.
Tisma is full of royal herons again
                         reflected in its mirrors.
It has many little starlings, *piches*, *güises*, widgets.
     The plant life has benefited too.
The armadillos are very happy with this government.
     We will restore our forests, rivers, lagoons.
We will decontaminate Lake Managua.
Not only humans longed for liberation.

Acabándose la tortuga caguama.

El pez-sierra del Gran Lago acabándolo José Somoza.

En peligro de extinción el tigrillo de la selva,
    su suave piel color de selva,
y el puma, el danto en las montañas
            (como los campesinos en las montañas).

¡Y pobre el Río Chiquito! Su desgracia,
la de todo el país. Reflejado en sus aguas el somocismo.

El Río Chiquito de León, alimentado de manantiales
de cloacas, desechos de fábricas de jabón y curtiembres,
agua blanca de fábricas de jabón, roja la de las curtiembres;
plásticos en el lecho, bacinillas, hierros sarrosos. Eso
nos dejó el somocismo.

(Hay que verlo otra vez bonito y claro cantando hacia el
    mar.)

Y al lago de Managua todas las aguas negras de Managua
y los desechos químicos.

    Y allá por Solentiname, en la isla La Zanata
un gran cerro blanco y hediondo de esqueletos de pez-sierra.

Pero ya respiraron los pez-sierra y el tiburón de agua dulce.

Tisma está llena otra vez de garzas reales
                    reflejadas en sus espejos.

Tiene muchos zanatillos, piches, güises, zarcetas.

    La flora también se ha beneficiado.

Los cusucos andan muy contentos con este gobierno.

    Recuperaremos los bosques, ríos, lagunas.

Vamos a descontaminar el lago de Managua.

La liberación no sólo la ansiaban los humanos.

All ecology groaned for it also. The revolution
is also one of lakes, rivers, trees, animals.

translated by Marc Zimmerman

Toda la ecología gemía. La revolución
es también de lagos, ríos, árboles, animales.

HEGEL IN THE CARIBBEAN

Papa Hegel is sovereign sap
in philosophy's elm:
his German philosopher words
still travel triumphantly
around beings, birds
and life's beautiful things,
while his beacon remains blind
to the shipwreck of Blacks in the Caribbean.
    Is that why the sea
      is a tragic poet?
Papa Hegel knows by heart,
like his pulpit, the dialectics
of existence and appearance in plantation
society: master and slave
          settler/native
          saint Christian/loa voodoo
          French/Creole
          White/Black/Mulatto
yet his words make shadows around
the problems of mask and truth.
    Is that why my life
      isn't a glass staircase?
Papa Hegel has a carpenter's strong
loud hands to artificially light
the laws and secrets of humanity's

HEGEL AUX CARAÏBES

Papa Hegel est sève souveraine
dans l'orme de la philosophie :
ses mots de philosophe allemand
voyagent encore en triomphe
autour des êtres, des oiseaux
et des choses belles de la vie,
tandis que son phare reste aveugle
au naufrage des Noirs de la mer caraïbe.
    Est-ce pour cela que la mer
      est un poète tragique ?
Papa Hegel connaît par coeur,
comme son pupitre, la dialectique
de l'être et du paraître en société
de plantation : maître et esclave
      colon/indigène
      saint chrétien/loa vaudou
      français/créole
      blanc/noir/mulâtre
pourtant ses mots font des ombres autour
des problèmes du masque et de la vérité.
    Est-ce pour cela que ma vie
      n'est pas un escalier de verre ?
Papa Hegel a de fortes mains voyantes
de menuisier pour éclairer a giorno
lois et secrets de la grande histoire

great history, but he has no brother's
eyes for the bleak veins running
in panic in the wood of black woe.
    Is that why, my negress,
      we eat and dance in the kitchen
      at evening parties in the West?

translated by Hélène Cardona

des humanités, mais il n'a pas d'yeux de frère
pour les veines qui courent, affolées,
désolées, dans le bois du malheur noir.
    Est-ce pour cela, ma négresse,
        qu'on mange et danse à la cuisine
        quand c'est soir de fête en Occident?

HERE WE ARE

Here we are the black mothers
turning to stone
like a rare specimen
from other ages.
Though these words
cannot change
the decisions of the men
who keep the people
in shadow.
Here we are the powerful women
surrounded by torturers
reduced to ashes
by the hand of man.
Where will our family bloom
if they contaminate life
in the Pacific
and explode outer space
shatter the air with imaginary dragons
if they upset the balance of the Polar snows
and also the depths of the earth?
Where to feed the children's smiles
with dead fish, dead vegetables, dead air
poisoned food
hair, skin, eye color
poisoned

AQUÍ ESTAMOS

Aquí estamos las madres negras
petrificándonos
como un raro ejemplar
de otras edades.
Sin que estas palabras
puedan cambiar
las decisiones de los hombres
que mantienen los pueblos
en la sombra.
Aquí estamos las mujeres poderosas
rodeadas de atormentadores
reducidas a cenizas
por la mano del hombre.
¿Dónde va a florecer nuestra familia
si se contamina la vida
en el Pacífico
y hacen estallar el espacio
rompen el aire de dragones imaginarios
si desequilibran las nieves de los Polos
y también las profundidades de la tierra?
Dónde alimentar la sonrisa de los hijos
con peces muertos, vegetales muertos, aire muerto
alimento envenenado
cabellos, piel, el color de los ojos
envenenado

the joy of living poisoned.
Though none of my words
can change anything.
Here I disintegrate
having neither taken part
nor been a poet bound
to any one of those
destructive
minds of my generations upon the earth.

translated by Jessica Powell

la alegría de vivir envenenada.
Sin que ninguna de mis palabras
pueda cambiar nada.
Aquí me desintegro
sin haber tomado parte
ni ser poeta comprometida
con cualquiera de esas mentes
destructoras
de mis generaciones sobre la tierra.

THE POOR

The poor are many
and so
it's impossible to forget them.

Surely
at dawn
they see
many buildings
where they'd
like to live with their children.

They can
carry on their shoulders
the coffin of a star.

They can
destroy the air like furious birds,
to blot out the sun.

But unaware of their treasures
they come and go through mirrors of blood;
they walk and die slowly.

That's why
it's impossible to forget them.

translated by Jack Hirschman

LOS POBRES

Los pobres son muchos
y por eso
es imposible olvidarlos.

Seguramente
ven
en los amaneceres
múltiples edificios
donde ellos
quisieran habitar con sus hijos.

Pueden
llevar en hombros
el féretro de una estrella.

Pueden
destruir el aire como aves furiosas,
nublar el sol.

Pero desconociendo sus tesoros
entran y salen por espejos de sangre;
caminan y mueren despacio.

Por eso
es imposible olvidarlos.

ESTADIO CHILE (HOW HARD IT IS TO SING)

There are five thousand of us here
in this small part of the city.
We are five thousand.
I wonder how many we are in all
in the cities and in the whole country?
Here alone
are ten thousand hands which plant seeds
and make the factories run.
How much humanity
exposed to hunger, cold, panic, pain,
moral pressure, terror and insanity?

Six of us were lost
as if into starry space.
One dead, another beaten as I could never have believed
a human being could be beaten.
The other four wanted to end their terror
one jumping into nothingness,
another beating his head against a wall,
but all with the fixed stare of death.
What horror the face of fascism creates!
They carry out their plans with knife-like precision.
Nothing matters to them.
To them, blood equals medals,
slaughter is an act of heroism.

ESTADIO CHILE (CANTO QUÉ MAL ME SALES)

Somos cinco mil aquí
en esta pequeña parte de la ciudad.
Somos cinco mil.
¿Cuántos somos en total
en las ciudades y en todo el país?
Sólo aquí,
diez mil manos que siembran
y hacen andar las fábricas.
Cuánta humanidad
con hambre, frío, pánico, dolor,
presión moral, terror y locura.

Seis de los nuestros se perdieron
en el espacio de las estrellas.
Uno muerto, un golpeado como jamás creí
se podría golpear a un ser humano.
Los otros cuatro quisieron quitarse
todos los temores,
uno saltando al vacío,
otro golpeándose la cabeza contra un muro
pero todos con la mirada fija en la muerte.
¡Qué espanto produce el rostro del fascismo!
Llevan a cabo sus planes con precisión artera
sin importarles nada.
La sangre para ellos son medallas.

Oh God, is this the world that you created,
for this your seven days of wonder and work?
Within these four walls only a number exists
which does not progress,
which slowly will wish more and more for death.

But suddenly my conscience awakes
and I see that this tide has no heartbeat,
only the pulse of machines
and the military showing their midwives' faces
full of sweetness.
Let Mexico, Cuba and the world
cry out against this atrocity!
We are ten thousand hands
which can produce nothing.
How many of us in the whole country?
The blood of our President, our compañero,
will strike with more strength than bombs and machine guns!
So will our fist strike again!

How hard it is to sing
when I must sing of horror.
Horror which I am living,
horror which I am dying.
To see myself among so much
and so many moments of infinity
in which silence and screams
are the end of my song.

La matanza es un acto de heroísmo.
¿Es este el mundo que creaste, Dios mío?
¿Para esto tus siete días de asombro y de trabajo?
En estas cuatro murallas sólo existe un número
que no progresa.
Que lentamente querrá más la muerte.

Pero de pronto me golpea la consciencia
y veo esta marea sin latido
y veo el pulso de las máquinas
y los militares mostrando su rostro de matrona
llena de dulzura.
¿Y México, Cuba y el mundo?
¡Que griten esta ignominia!
Somos diez mil manos
menos que no producen.
¿Cuántos somos en toda la patria?
La sangre del compañero Presidente
golpea más fuerte que bombas y metrallas.
Así golpeará nuestro puño nuevamente.

Canto, qué mal me sales
cuando tengo que cantar espanto.
Espanto como el que vivo
como el que muero, espanto.
De verme entre tantos y tantos
momentos de infinito
en que el silencio y el grito

What I see, I have never seen.
What I have felt and what I feel
will give birth to the moment . . .

translated by Joan Jara

son las metas de este canto.
Lo que veo nunca vi.
Lo que he sentido y lo que siento
harán brotar el momento . . .

ACT

In the name of those washing others' clothes
(and cleansing others' filth from the whiteness)

In the name of those caring for others' children
(and selling their labor power
in the form of maternal love and humiliations)

In the name of those living in another's house
(which isn't even a kind belly but a tomb or jail)

In the name of those eating others' crumbs
(and chewing them still with the feeling of a thief)

In the name of those living on others' land
(the houses and factories and shops
streets cities and towns
rivers lakes volcanoes and mountains
always belong to others
and that's why the cops and the guards are there
guarding them against us)

ACTA

En nombre de quienes lavan ropa ajena
(y expulsan de la blancura la mugre ajena)

En nombre de quienes cuidan hijos ajenos
(y venden su fuerza de trabajo
en forma de amor maternal y humillaciones)

En nombre de quienes habitan en vivienda ajena
(que ya no es vientre amable sino una tumba o cárcel)

En nombre de quienes comen mendrugos ajenos
(y aún los mastican con sentimiento de ladrón)

En nombre de quienes viven en un país ajeno
(las casas y las fábricas y los comercios
y las calles y las ciudades y los pueblos
y los ríos y los lagos y los volcanes y los montes
son siempre de otros
y por eso está allí la policía y la guardia
cuidándolos contra nosotros)

In the name of those who have nothing but
hunger exploitation disease
a thirst for justice and water
persecution and condemnations
loneliness abandonment oppression and death

I accuse private property
of depriving us of everything

translated by Jack Hirschman

En nombre de quienes lo único que tienen
es hambre explotación enfermedades
sed de justicia y de agua
persecuciones condenas
soledad abandono opresión muerte

Yo acuso a la propiedad privada
de privarnos de todo

I KNOW

I know.
I'll never be more than a
warrior for love.
      I'm situated somewhere
on the erotic left.
Lobbing bullet after bullet
against the system.
Losing power and time
by preaching an outdated gospel.

I'm going to end up like that other crazy one
      who was left
discarded in the mountains.

But since my struggle
is not a politics that serves men
they will never publish my diary
nor build industries for popular consumption
of posters
and pendants with my photo.

translated by Barbara Paschke

YA SÉ

Ya sé.
Nunca voy a ser más que una
guerrillera del amor.
          Estoy situada algo así
como a la izquierda erótica.
Soltando bala tras bala
contra el sistema.
Perdiendo fuerza y tiempo
en predicar un evangelio trasnochado.

Voy a terminar como aquel otro loco
          que se quedó
tirado en la sierra.

Pero como mi lucha
no es política que sirva a los hombres
jamás publicarán mi diario
ni construirán industrias de consumo popular
de carteles
y colgajos con mis fotografías.

THE ONLY WOMAN

The only woman that she can be
is the one who knows the sun of her life begins now

the one who sheds not tears but darts
to sow the barbed wire of her territory

the one who begs for nothing
who speaks her mind, holds her head up and shakes her body
who is tender without shame and hard without hatred

the one who unlearns the alphabet of submission
who walks tall and true

the one who does not fear solitude because she's always been alone
who lets the grotesque howls of violence pass her by

and she does it with grace
the one who frees herself through the fullness of love
the one who loves

the only woman, the only one that she can be
is the one who, aching and clean, decides for herself
to leave her prehistory behind.

translated by William O'Daly

LA ÚNICA MUJER

La única mujer que puede ser
es la que sabe que el sol para su vida empieza ahora

la que no derrama lágrimas sino dardos para
sembrar la alambrada de su territorio

la que no comete ruegos
la que opina y levanta su cabeza y agita su cuerpo
y es tierna sin vergüenza y dura sin odios

la que desaprende el alfabeto de la sumisión
y camina erguida

la que no le teme a la soledad porque siempre ha estado sola
la que deja pasar los alaridos grotescos de la violencia

y la ejecuta con gracia
la que se libera en el amor pleno
la que ama

la única mujer que puede ser la única
es la que dolorida y limpia decide por sí misma
salir de su prehistoria.

HIGH TREASON

I don't love my homeland.
Its abstract splendor
is beyond my grasp.
Still (though it sounds bad)
I'd give my life
for ten places there,
certain folks,
ports, forests, deserts, fortresses,
a city in ruins, ashen, monstrous,
various historical figures,
mountains
—and three or four rivers.

translated by Katherine M. Hedeen and Víctor Rodríguez Núñez

ALTA TRAICIÓN

No amo mi patria.
Su fulgor abstracto
es inasible.
Pero (aunque suene mal)
daría la vida
por diez lugares suyos,
cierta gente,
puertos, bosques, desiertos, fortalezas,
una ciudad deshecha, gris, monstruosa,
varias figuras de su historia,
montañas
—y tres o cuatro ríos.

LIFE IS KILLING ME

Political terror no longer pursues me
with its laser beam,
my fellow man does not love me
with his stick and electric prod.

The Universal Declaration of Human Rights
no longer offends me,
the bomb does not keep me awake,
not even the gunshots
from some little war in Africa or Europe,
    what difference does it make!

Walls fall,
laments grow.
And hatred returns
with its violent angels.

The South is still where it was.
We don't misbehave
    (it's obvious)
and we're all so content,
constitutionally.

LA VIDA ME ESTÁ MATANDO

Ya no me persigue el terror político
con su rayo láser,
ni los prójimos me aman
con su palo y su picana eléctrica.

Ya no me ofende la Declaración Universal
de los Derechos Humanos,
ni la bomba me quita el sueño,
ni siquiera los disparos
de una guerrita en Africa o Europa,
    ¡qué más da!

Caen los muros,
crecen los lamentos.
Y el odio vuelve
con sus ángeles violentos.

El Sur sigue donde estaba.
No nos portamos mal
    (es evidente)
y todos tan contentos,
constitucionalmente.

This life is too much for me
with its nicotine,
with its heart attack and its cancer,
with its fear of AIDS and syringes.
Only love
and poetry
can be mine
when no one seems to care anymore about
love
and
poetry.

translated by Jessica Powell

Esta vida me sobra
con su nicotina,
con su infarto y su cáncer,
con su miedo al sida y las jeringas.
Sólo el amor
y la poesía
pueden ser míos
cuando a nadie parece ya importarle
el amor
y
la poesía.

BLACK WOMAN

Still I smell the foam of the sea which they made me cross.
The night, I cannot remember it.
Not even the ocean itself could remember it.
But I do not forget the first gannet I made out.
High, the clouds, like innocent eyewitnesses.
Perhaps I have forgotten my lost coast, or my ancestral tongue.
They left me here and here I have lived.
And because I worked like a beast,
here I was born again.
To how many Mandinga epopeias did I try to have recourse.

I rebelled.

His Honour bought me in a square.
I embroidered His Honour's coat and gave birth to a son for him.
My son had no name.
And His Honour, he died at the hands of an impeccable English lord.

I walked.

This is the land in which I suffered beatings and floggings.
I rowed the length of all its rivers.
Under its sun I sowed, I reaped and I did not eat the harvests.
For a house I had a shack.
I myself brought stones to build it,
but I sang to the natural beat of the national birds.

MUJER NEGRA

Todavía huelo la espuma del mar que me hicieron atravesar.
La noche, no puedo recordarla.
Ni el mismo océano podría recordarla.
Pero no olvido el primer alcatraz que divisé.
Altas, las nubes, como inocentes testigos presenciales.
Acaso no he olvidado ni mi costa perdida, ni mi lengua ancestral.
Me dejaron aquí y aquí he vivido.
Y porque trabajé como una bestia,
aquí volví a nacer.
A cuanta epopeya mandinga intenté recurrir.

Me rebelé.

Su Merced me compró en una plaza.
Bordé la casaca de su Merced y un hijo macho le parí.
Mi hijo no tuvo nombre.
Y su Merced murió a manos de un impecable lord inglés.

Anduve.

Esta es la tierra donde padecí bocabajos y azotes.
Bogué a lo largo de todos sus ríos.
Bajo su sol sembré, recolecté y las cosechas no comí.
Por casa tuve un barracón.
Yo misma traje piedras para edificarlo,
pero canté al natural compás de los pájaros nacionales.

I rose up.

In this same land I touched the humid blood
and the rotted bones of many others,
brought to it, or not, the same as I.
By then I did not imagine the way to Guinea any more.
Was it to Guinea? To Benin? Was it to Madagascar? Or to
     Cape Verde?

I worked much harder.

I laid better foundations for my millennial song and my hope.
Here I built my world.

I went off to the mountains.

My real independence was the Palenque
and I rode among the troops of Maceo.

Only a century later,
together with my descendants,
from a blue mountain,

I came down from the Sierra
.

Me sublevé.

En esta tierra toqué la sangre húmeda
y los huesos podridos de muchos otros,
traídos a ella, o no, igual que yo.
Ya nunca más imaginé el camino a Guinea.
¿Era a Guinea? ¿A Benín? ¿Era a Madagascar? ¿O a
    Cabo Verde?

Trabajé mucho más.

Fundé mejor mi canto milenario y mi esperanza.
Aquí construí mi mundo.

Me fui al monte.

Mi real independencia fue el palenque
y cabalgué entre las tropas de Maceo.

Sólo un siglo más tarde,
junto a mis descendientes,
desde una azul montaña,

bajé de la Sierra

to put an end to capitalists and usurers,
to generals and bourgeois.
Now I am: Only today do we have and create.
Nothing is outside our reach.
Ours the land.
Ours the sea and the sky.
Ours magic and the chimera.
My equals, here I watch them dance
around the tree we planted for communism.
Its prodigious wood already resounds.

translated by Jean Andrews

para acabar con capitales y usureros,
con generales y burgueses.
Ahora soy: sólo hoy tenemos y creamos.
Nada nos es ajeno.
Nuestra la tierra.
Nuestros el mar y el cielo.
Nuestras la magia y la quimera.
Iguales míos, aquí los veo bailar
alrededor del árbol que plantamos para el comunismo.
Su pródiga madera ya resuena.

NIGHT NEVER SLEEPS IN THE EYES OF WOMEN

In memory of Beatriz Nascimento

Night never sleeps
in the eyes of women
the maternal moon, akin to us
in watchful vigil, watches
over our memory.

Night never sleeps
in the eyes of women
there are more eyes than slumber
where suspended tears
punctuate the lapses
of our sodden remembrances.

Night never sleeps
in the eyes of women
open vaginas
preserve and cast out life
wherein Ainás, Nzingas, Ngambeles
and other moon daughters
remove from them and us
our chalices of tears.

A NOITE NÃO ADORMECE NOS OLHOS DAS MULHERES

Em memória de Beatriz Nascimento

A noite não adormece
nos olhos das mulheres
a lua fêmea, semelhante nossa,
em vigília atenta vigia
a nossa memória.

A noite não adormece
nos olhos das mulheres
há mais olhos que sono
onde lágrimas suspensas
virgulam o lapso
de nossas molhadas lembranças.

A noite não adormece
nos olhos das mulheres
vaginas abertas
retêm e expulsam a vida
donde Ainás, Nzingas, Ngambeles
e outras meninas luas
afastam delas e de nós
os nossos cálices de lágrimas.

Night will never sleep
in female eyes
for from our woman-blood
from our memorious liquid
in each drop that flows
a thread, invisible and tonic,
patiently weaves the web
of our millenary resistance.

translated by Megan Coxe

A noite não adormecerá
jamais nos olhos das fêmeas
pois do nosso sangue-mulher
de nosso líquido lembradiço
em cada gota que jorra
um fio invisível e tônico
pacientemente cose a rede
de nossa milenar resistência.

BATTLE CRY OF ONE WHO NEVER WENT TO WAR

I never saw, on the railings of a bridge
The sweet woman with Assyrian eyes
Threading a needle
As if to mend the river.
Nor lonely women waiting in the villages
For the war to pass like another season.
I never went to war, nor do I need to,
Because as a boy
I always asked how to go to war
And a nurse, beautiful as an albatross,
A nurse who ran down the long hallways
Screamed in the caw of a bird, without looking at me:
You're already in it, kid, you're in it.
I never went to the land of hangars,
I've never been a flag bearer, a hussar, a muzhik on the Steppes.
I never traveled by hot-air balloon over thorny countries
Populated with troops and with beer.
I haven't written love letters from the trenches like Ungaretti.
I haven't seen the sun of death burning in Japan
Nor have I seen men in tall collars
Splitting the world up amongst themselves in a game of cards.
I never went to war, nor do I need to,
In order to see soldiers washing white insignias,
And then hear them speak of peace
At the feet of a legion of statues.

translated by Emily Toder

ARENGA DE UNO QUE NO FUE A LA GUERRA

Nunca vi en las barandas de un puente
A la dulce mujer con ojos de asiria
Enhebrando una aguja
Como si fuera a remendar el río.
Ni mujeres solas esperando en las aldeas
A que pase la guerra como si fuera otra estación.
Nunca fui a la guerra, ni falta que me hace,
Porque de niño
Siempre pregunté cómo ir a la guerra
Y una enfermera bella como un albatros,
Una enfermera que corría por largos pasillos
Gritó con graznido de ave sin mirarme:
Ya estás en ella, muchacho, estás en ella.
Nunca he ido al país de los hangares,
Nunca he sido abanderado, húsar, mujik de alguna estepa.
Nunca viajé en globo por erizados países
Poblados de tropa y de cerveza.
No he escrito como Ungaretti cartas de amor en las trincheras.
No he visto el sol de la muerte ardiendo en el Japón
Ni he visto hombres de largo cuello
Repartiéndose la tierra en un juego de barajas.
Nunca fui a la guerra, ni falta que me hace,
Para ver la soldadesca lavando los blancos estandartes,
Y luego oírlos hablar de la paz
Al pie de la legión de las estatuas.

STRIKE

I want a strike where we all walk out.
A strike of arms, of legs, of hair,
A strike born from every body.

I want a strike
of workers   of doves
of drivers   of flowers
of technicians   of children
of doctors   of women

I want a giant strike,
that extends even to love.
A strike that brings everything to a halt,
the clock   the factories
the yard   the schools
the bus   the hospitals
the highway   the ports

A strike of eyes, of hands, and of kisses.
A strike where it is forbidden to breathe,
a strike where silence is born
            so you can hear the footsteps
            of the tyrant as he walks away.

translated by Mark Eisner

HUELGA

Quiero una huelga donde vayamos todos.
Una huelga de brazos, de piernas, de cabellos,
Una huelga naciendo de cada cuerpo.

Quiero una huelga
de obreros   de palomas
de choferes   de flores
de técnicos   de niños
de médicos   de mujeres

Quiero una huelga grande,
que hasta el amor alcance.
Una huelga donde todo se detenga,
el reloj   las fábricas
el plantel   los colegios
el bus   los hospitales
la carretera   los puertos

Una huelga de ojos, de manos y de besos.
Una huelga donde respirar no sea permitido,
una huelga donde nazca el silencio
            para oír los pasos
            del tirano que se marcha.

AUTOGRAPH

The poets of yesteryear
were asked, by and large, to write acrostics.
But now,
when rancor is the only word
I know how to pronounce,
with what winding calligraphy
(Palmer script?)
will I manage to transmit the profound contempt
that lives within me?
I grit my teeth, and carry on,
free of all Romanticism:
my work consists
of writing obituaries
two or three times a year.
For those who struggle, too,
with desolation and shame:
such could be the grandiloquent dedication,
and then the verbose fourteen verses,
laden with syrup.
What to say to you
that they haven't said to you already,
the serving girl, the maiden aunt:
resignation and experience.
As for the books, wipe away the dust;
organize the closet, and get those plants

AUTÓGRAFO

A los poetas de antes
les pedían, generalmente, un acróstico.
Sólo que ahora,
cuando el rencor es la única palabra
que sé pronunciar,
¿con qué enrevesada caligrafía
(letra palmer, ¿no?)
lograré transmitir el profundo desprecio
que hay en mí?
Aprieto los dientes, y sigo,
exento de todo romanticismo:
mi tarea consiste
en redactar notas necrológicas
dos o tres veces al año.
A quien se debate, también,
entre el abandono y la lástima:
tal podría ser la grandilocuente dedicatoria,
y luego los prolijos catorce versos,
llenos de almíbar.
Qué decirte
que no te hubieran dicho ya,
la muchacha de la casa, la tía solterona:
resignación y experiencia.
A los libros, quítales el polvo;
ordena el closet, y consigue aquellas matas

you've always wanted for the apartment's
balcony.
(The tragedy, keep it secret.)

translated by Emily Toder

que siempre has querido para el balcón del apartamento.

(La tragedia consérvala en secreto).

THE EARTH IS A SATELLITE OF THE MOON

Apollo 2 cost more than Apollo 1
Apollo 1 cost plenty.

Apollo 3 cost more than Apollo 2
Apollo 2 cost more than Apollo 1
Apollo 1 cost plenty.

Apollo 4 cost more than Apollo 3
Apollo 3 cost more than Apollo 2
Apollo 2 cost more than Apollo 1
Apollo 1 cost plenty.

Apollo cost a heap, but no one cared
because the astronauts were Protestants
and they read the Bible from the moon
astounding and exhilarating all Christians
and upon their return Pope Paul VI gave them his blessing.

Apollo 9 cost more than all of them put together
along with Apollo 1 that cost plenty.

LA TIERRA ES UN SATÉLITE DE LA LUNA

El Apolo 2 costó más que el Apolo 1
el Apolo 1 costó bastante.

El Apolo 3 costó más que el Apolo 2
el Apolo 2 costó más que el Apolo 1
el Apolo 1 costó bastante.

El Apolo 4 costó más que el Apolo 3
el Apolo 3 costó más que el Apolo 2
el Apolo 2 costó más que el Apolo 1
el Apolo 1 costó bastante.

El Apolo costó un montón, pero no se sintió
porque los astronautas eran protestantes
y desde la luna leyeron la Biblia
maravillando y alegrando a todos los cristianos
y a la venida el papa Paulo VI les dio la bendición.

El Apolo 9 costó más que todos juntos
junto con el Apolo 1 que costó bastante.

The great-grandparents of the Acahualinca people were less
   hungry than the grandparents.
The great-grandparents died from hunger.
The grandparents of the Acahualinca people were less
   hungry than the parents.
The grandparents died from hunger.
The parents of the Acahualinca people were less hungry than
   the children of the people from there.
The parents died from hunger.
The Acahualinca people were less hungry than the children
   of the people from there.
The children of the Acahualinca people were not born
   because of hunger
and were hungry to be born, to die from hunger.
Blessed are the poor for they shall inherit the moon.

translated by Barbara Paschke

Los bisabuelos de la gente de Acahualinca tenían menos
hambre que los abuelos.
Los bisabuelos se murieron de hambre.
Los abuelos de la gente de Acahualinca tenían menos hambre
que los padres.
Los abuelos murieron de hambre.
Los padres de la gente de Acahualinca tenían menos hambre
que los hijos de la gente de allí.
Los padres se murieron de hambre.
La gente de Acahualinca tiene menos hambre que los hijos
de la gente de allí.
Los hijos de la gente de Acahualinca no nacen por hambre,
y tienen hambre de nacer, para morirse de hambre.
Bienaventurados los pobres porque de ellos será la luna.

WITH RESPECT TO CERTAIN ACTIVITIES OF DOVES

From Lincoln to Lenin,
from Bolívar to Zapata,
the statues of the masculine
heroes of the Earth,
the matriots,
are already profaned forever
with the odorless gray that adorns their heads.

It is the peaceful doves that are responsible
for this attack on the virile temple of our fatherland,
doves that vindicate (wanting to make us believe
they don't know what they are doing) the place
the useless statues occupy in the soul of the people—
statues raised by the hunger of the politician
to the illustrious male that serves them as bait.
Thus they fill these people's brains
with drooling hopes and incongruent promises.

Is this not what the doves think
coming in and perching on the cranium of the statue,
there carrying out certain activity that destroys
the idea we had, so sacred,
about the heroes of the fatherland?

translated by Tom Jones

CON RESPECTO A CIERTA ACTIVIDAD DE LAS PALOMAS

Desde Lincoln a Lenín,
de Bolívar a Zapata,
las estatuas de los héroes
masculinos de la tierra,
los matriotas,
profanadas están ya para siempre
con el gris inodoro que le adorna las cabezas.

Responsables de este ataque al templo varonil de nuestra patria
son las pacíficas palomas
que vindican—quieren hacernos creer que sin saberlo—
el lugar que ocupan en el alma de la gente,
las inútiles estatuas levantadas por el hambre del político
al ilustre varón que le sirve de carnada.
Así le llenan a este pueblo la mollera
de babosas esperanzas y promesas incongruentes.

¿No será eso lo que piensan las palomas
al venir y posarse sobre el cráneo de la estatua
y allí llevan a cabo cierta actividad que nos destruye
la idea que teníamos, tan sagrada, de los héroes de la patria?

THIS IS MY COUNTRY RISING

This is my country rising
With the sun's luminous fist
It put sandals of justice on its feet
And its voice trumpeted the truth of times
The ears opened out
The eyes saw the nourishing word
It sings *péyi la sé tan nou*
And the leaves respond in unison
To the song of its dew
Men and women walk with an even step
Sing in even voice
The drums cross the street
They carry the beautiful weather on their shoulders
They illuminate life despite the agony of shadows
The young came to unearth their dreams
Country risen
Country cleansed
Looking forward to the tenderness of tomorrow
In revolt against greed
Between anger and love
Opening its roots like a new hand
Reconciled with its cry
And its harvest of stars
Out of the torpor of mangroves
The immobility of powerless statues

VOILÀ MON PAYS QUI SE LÈVE

Voilà mon pays qui se lève
Avec le poing lumineux du soleil
Il a mis aux pieds des sandales de justice
Et sa voix a claironné la vérité des temps
Les oreilles se sont ouvertes
Les yeux ont vu la parole nourricière
Il chante péyi la sé tan nou
Et les feuilles répondent en chœur
Au chant de sa rosée
Les hommes et les femmes marchent d'un pas égal
Chantent d'une voix égale
Les tambours ont traversé la rue
Ils portent le beau temps sur leurs épaules
Ils éclairent la vie malgré la souffrance des ombres
Les jeunes sont venus déterrer leurs rêves
Pays levé
Pays lavé
En marche vers la tendresse des lendemains
En révolte contre les profitations
Entre colère et amour
Ouvrant ses racines comme une main nouvelle
Réconcilié avec son cri
Et sa récolte d'étoiles
Sorti de la torpeur des mangroves
De l'immobilité des statues impuissantes

My country rose at once
With a single breath of forbidden tornado
With a single wave of ripening memory
Country risen
Country cleansed
And it said enough
Let Guadeloupe through!

translated by Hélène Cardona

Mon pays s'est levé d'un seul coup
D'un seul souffle de tornade interdite
D'une seule houle de mémoire murissante
Pays levé
Pays lavé
Et il a dit assez
Laissez passer la Guadeloupe!

THE BEACHES OF CHILE V

> Chile did not find one just man on
> its beaches stoned no one could
> cleanse his hands of these wounds

Because stoned not one just man could be found on those
beaches but the homeland's stained wounds   somber   full of
sores as if they themselves shut with their shadows their eyes

    i. Clinging to his ribs he could be seen kissing himself

    ii. Never had anyone heard a more ardent plea than the one
         from his lips wringing himself against his arms

    iii. Never had someone seen abysses of such depths than the
         marks of his own teeth on his arms   convulsed   as if
         he wanted to devour his own self in that despairing

Because stoned Chile did not find one just man on her beaches
but the shadows of their own selves on air afloat   of death
as if in this world there were not one person who could make
them live again before their eyes

LAS PLAYAS DE CHILE V

Chile no encontró un solo justo en
sus playas   apedreados   nadie pudo
lavarse las manos de estas heridas

Porque apedreados nadie encontró un solo justo en esas playas
sino las heridas maculadas de la patria   sombrías   llagadas
como si ellas mismas les cerraran con sus sombras los ojos

    i.   Aferrado a las cuadernas se vio besándose a sí mismo

   ii.   Nunca nadie escuchó ruego más ardiente que el de sus
        labios estrujándose contra sus brazos

  iii.   Nunca alguien vio abismos más profundos que las marcas
        de sus propios dientes en los brazos   convulso   como
        si quisiera devorarse a sí mismo en esa desesperada

Porque apedreado Chile no encontró un solo justo en sus playas
sino las sombras de ellos mismos flotantes sobre el aire   de
muerte   como si en este mundo no hubiera nadie que los pudiera
revivir ante sus ojos

iv. But their wounds could be the just man of the beaches of Chile

v. We would be then the beach that raised up a just man for them from their wounds

vi. Only there would all the inhabitants of Chile have been made one until being themselves the just man they beat   swollen waiting for himself on the beach

Where stoned Chile saw its own self receive itself like a just man on her beaches so that we would be there the stones that to the air we threw   sick   reclining   cleansing our hands of the open wounds of my homeland

translated by Anna Deeny Morales

iv. Pero sus heridas podrían ser el justo de las playas de
Chile

v. Nosotros seríamos entonces la playa que les alzó un justo
desde sus heridas

vi. Sólo allí todos los habitantes de Chile se habrían hecho
uno hasta ser ellos el justo que golpearon   tumefactos
esperándose en la playa

Donde apedreado Chile se vio a sí mismo recibirse como un justo
en sus playas para que nosotros fuésemos allí las piedras que al aire
lanzamos   enfermos   yacentes   limpiándonos las manos de las
heridas abiertas de mi patria

DAGUERREOTYPE OF A MOTHER

You understood everything perfectly:
the epoch, the limits, your place.

Your intelligence was wasted on petty details.
You invested your talent in managing the pantry,
organizing the household,
your imagination confined
to common household work.

How you put up with it, kept your mouth shut,
sank your tears before they surfaced!

But your dignity nourished my rebellion,
and your silence my will to speak out.

translated by George Evans

DAGUERROTIPO DE LA MADRE

Todo lo entendiste perfectamente:
la época, los límites, el lugar que ocupabas.

Tu inteligencia se desperdició en minucias.
Invertiste tu talento en administrar la despensa
y organizar el servicio de la casa.
Tu imaginación fue confinada a la vulgaridad
de lo doméstico.

¡Cómo resistías con los labios cerrados
y el llanto naufragaba antes de alcanzar tus ojos!

Pero tu dignidad nutrió mi rebeldía,
y tu silencio mi voluntad de hablar.

ROMEO AND I (A DIALECTICAL STORY AND, IPSO FACTO, ROMANTIC POEM)

[First Version, 1977]

I want to play with you.
Dad won't let me.
The Principal forbids it.
The Leftists are against me.

You call me
and I die to go.
Dad threatens me.
The Principal shouts an ultimatum at me.
The Leftists terrorize me.

I go out secretly,
looking for you,
but they find me.
Dad beats me up.
The Principal punishes me.
The Leftists attack me.

ROMEU E EU (CONTO DIALÉTICO E, IPSO FACTO, POEMA ROMÂNTICO)

[Primeira versão, 1977]

Eu quero brincar com você.
Papai não deixa.
O Diretor proíbe.
A Esquerda se opõe.

Você me chama
e eu morro de vontade.
Papai me ameaça.
O Diretor me intima.
A Esquerda me aterroriza.

Saio escondido,
procuro por você,
mas eles me acham.
Papai me bate.
O Diretor me põe de castigo.
A Esquerda atenta contra mim.

I keep waiting,
you seek me,
we meet in the dark,
they catch us in the act.
Dad throws me out.
The Principal sends me to reformatory.
The Leftists kidnap me.

I run away and survive,
but you're not free.
You are loyal to your father.
Disciplined by your Principal.
Indoctrinated by the Leftists.

I live alone, you are a prisoner,
and we cannot play together.
They castrate our childhood
because you're like me,
your will is like mine,
but they force us to grow differently.

translated by Akira Nishimura

Fico esperando,
você me procura,
nos encontramos no escuro,
nos pegam em flagrante.
Papai me expulsa.
O Diretor me interna.
A Esquerda me seqüestra.

Escapo e sobrevivo,
mas você não está livre.
É filho de seu Papai.
Disciplinado ao seu Diretor.
Prosélito da sua Esquerda.

Vivo solitário, você prisioneiro,
e não podemos brincar.
Castram nossa infância
porque você é igual a mim,
sua vontade igual à minha,
mas nos fazem diferentes.

FIRST OUR SELK'NAM BROTHERS AND SISTERS (WERE) DISAPPEARED. MAPUCHE BROTHERS AND SISTERS, THEY WANT THE SAME THING FOR US

Here we are, brothers and sisters
    swans with outspread wings
perfect targets for the hunter
We ask for nothing more than wind, the final wind
a breath for the flight that awaits
We are far away: will it be too much to ask
    of these aged wings?
But the flock swells
Take wing, little swans!
gliding above the earth, the evening
    will be returned to us
(and isn't it evening, like old age,
when daytime and humankind alike
    hope to die in peace?)

The ocean wind blows in a far-off country,
but we do not forget
the scent of the canelo and arrayán trees
that once filled our lungs

KUYFI AFI IÑ PU PEÑI KA LAMGEN SELK'NAM. IÑCHIÑ IÑ MAPUCHEGEN KA FELEPEAY

Mvlelleyiñ ta faw, pu peñi / pu lamgen
     piwkan vnvlentu mvpv
eluñmaniyefiel kvllv pu tralkatufe
Neyen petu gillatuyiñ re af mvlewechi neyen
fey chi neyvn vgvmniyeel tayiñ mvpvam
Kamapu ta mvlelleyiñ, ¿alvyelley tayiñ puwam
     tvfachi pu wvntu mvpv?
Welu tremkvlelley lumpv vñvm
¡Mvpafvlleaymvn pichike pu piwpiw!
fey chi illaf, fey chi mapu wewlleayiñ
     wiñon afpun antv
(¿afpun antv amta gushke che no reke
fey chi antv ta che ayvn tvgkvlen layael?)

Kvrvfvlley zewma fvtra lafken kake mapu
welu iñchiñ guyvniyelayiñ
foye ta ñi wvrwan ka kollv mamvll
neyvntukukefel em ponon mew

145

In the city, canaries of ultimate truths
seek to capture our whispers
but in their cages, they only screech, screech
    with resentment

In memory, it's the southern wind that blows
though in truth
it's the northern wind slapping my cheek
(could anyone turn the other?)

Here comes the Puelche! The eastern wind
has arrived, the hour of our return
We will drink muzay, we will drink water
    from the springs
The mountains! But where is the green of the valley,
    and the nest of
solemn swans, on the verge of disappearing?

translated by Carl Fischer

Editors' note: This poem was originally written in Mapudungun and later
translated by the poet into Spanish. The English translation is based on
the Spanish version.

Waria mew, pu vlkantufe afpun feyentufal
ayvlellefuygvn tuñmayaetew tayiñ
   truwvr zugun
welu ñi pu malal, llazkvlefel egvn
   wirarkvlelleygvn / wirarkvlelleygvn

Kvpalelley willi kvrvf tayiñ pu mvllo mew
fey chi vyew −rvf ñi felen-
pikum kvrvf litraf niyeñmaenew ta ñi age
(¿kam mvley −iney chey- kagelu elael?)

¡Kvpalelley ta Puelche!, ti Puel kvrvf
puwlley antv ta wvñoam
Putulleafiyiñ muzay, wvf ko putulleafiyiñ
¡Wigkul mapu! Welu chew am karv
   Illaf Mapu ka fey chi zañe
kvmeke pu piwkan ¿kam zewma epeke
   ñamnaqlu?

CALIFORNIA APPLES

A California apple costs thirty centavos.
A tiny apple that arrived in our port
as contraband. It fits inside a fist.
(I give it to my daughter.)
It's sweet, yet acidic at the same time.
Like all true apples
it trades flavor for a price.
Young people will eat other things
recklessly.
The apple I don't try
(and will not try) and don't regret
was denied me at that age.
The agreement is sealed with other nations:
an apple in exchange for a heart.
Peace is made in foreign apples.
Who will take so many years of need and pain off our hands?
Apples astray in memory
weep green marrow.
Cavity by cavity, that seed
(in one's mouth) tastes of a corrupted land,
of desperation.
Tree of the apple prohibited back then
(and preferred today):
yours is poor fruit!

MANZANAS DE CALIFORNIA

Una manzana de California cuesta treinta centavos.
Una pequeña manzana llegada al puerto
de contrabando. Cabe en un puño.
(Se la doy a mi hija).
Es dulce, pero a la vez, ácida.
Como toda manzana verdadera
cuesta un sabor.
Los jóvenes comerán otras cosas
con imprudencia.
La manzana que no pruebo
(que no probaré) sin arrepentimientos
me fue negada entonces.
El convenio se cierra con ajenos,
se entrega por una manzana un corazón.
Hacen las paces con manzanas ajenas.
¿Quién nos quita tantos años de necesidades
y dolor?
Manzanas extraviadas en la memoria
supuran tuétanos verdes.
Cavidad por cavidad, esa semilla
(en la boca) sabe a tierra corrupta,
a desesperación.
Árbol de la manzana prohibida aquella vez
(y preferida hoy)
¡das frutos pobres!

Without the living apple in the basket,
where chewing is normally a gift,
how much do we cost now?
With no cures for this (political)
disease of eating when we're allowed.
I squeeze the apple against my fist
and bring it to my daughter
so she won't turn out like me.

translated by Kristin Dykstra

Sin la manzana viva en la cesta
con la normalidad de masticar un don
¿Cuánto costamos ahora?
Sin remedios contra esta enfermedad
(política) de comer cuando nos sea permitido.
Aprieto la manzana contra el puño
y se la llevo a ella
para que no sea como yo.

MY COUNTRY

to Armando

America: lie down quietly at my side
let your hair fall across my pillow,
press against my body
the stretched copper of your skin . . .
Let me tell you about David and Goliath,
about the books I wrote,
about the papers I threw out,
about each word: in verse or prose,
to know myself talking on and on
in the house of the stranger . . .
I know your word was the silence,
the repressed syllable,
the humiliated vowel.
America: lover-of-mine
I don't want you to fall asleep . . .
I want to tell you a myth,
let me, love, let me tell you
about David and Goliath.

translated by Idra Novey

PATRIA MÍA

a Armando

América: acuéstate callada al lado mío
deja caer tu pelo en mi almohada,
aprieta junto a mi cuerpo
el cobre estirado de tu piel . . .
Déjame contarte de David y Goliat,
de los libros que escribí,
de los papeles que tiré,
de cada palabra: verso y prosa,
para saberme siempre hablando
en la casa del extraño . . .
yo sé que tu palabra fue el silencio,
oprimida la sílaba
humillado el vocablo.
América: amante-mía
no quiero que te duermas . . .
quiero contarte un mito,
déjame, amor, que te hable
de David y Goliat.

THE ROUTINE APPEARANCES OF THE SUN

Everything here resides
in cleaning the other side of the stove
and reminding the Rosicrucian grandmother
of her Spanish deck, of her fondness for Lobsang Rampa
and of her gift for divination
in this house filled with night and garlic salt.
I am here
to clean the floor on Saturday mornings
and to forget about the dawn.
We have spoken of the routine appearances of the sun,
when for us women everything falls to pieces
because the sun sinks away on us
and no one teaches us to scream
because we are the shipwreck
of our one and only body full of life
and the ignorance of living it.

translated by Jessica Powell

LAS APARICIONES RUTINARIAS DEL SOL

Todo aquí reside
en lavar el otro lado de la estufa
y recordar a la abuela rosacruz
su baraja española, su afición a Lobsang Rampa
y su arte adivinatorio
en esta casa llena de noche y sal de ajo.
Aquí estoy
para limpiar el piso los sábados por la mañana
y olvidarme del amanecer.
Nos hemos hablado de las apariciones rutinarias del sol,
cuando a las mujeres todo se nos hace añicos
porque el sol se nos hunde
y nadie nos enseña a gritar
porque somos el naufragio
de nuestro único cuerpo lleno de vida
y de ignorancia por vivirla.

THE BRASILIADE (FRAGMENT)

I prostrate myself, I prostitute myself
as though I were the grass beneath your feet,
I drink from your mire,
I swim in your sewage,
I cut myself within,
I crucify myself on your posts

so that you will not be worthy of me,
Brasília!

. . . .

I, the one without an appointment book
I, the accessible one
I, the one who is never in a meeting
I, the one without power

I, the impotent one

translated by David William Foster

LA BRASILÍADA (FRAGMENTO)

Eu me prostro, me prostituo
como da tua grama,
bebo da tua lama,
nado em teu esgoto,
me corto por dentro,
me crucifico em teus postes

para que não me mereças,
brasília!

. . . .

eu, o sem-agenda
eu, o acessível
eu, que nunca estou em reunião
eu, o sem-poder

eu, o impotente

HUNGER HAPPENS

hunger
its persistent alchemy

a violent transmutation
in the ribs

to have a man alive between its fingers
to throw him toward death

hunger is a death
that acts like it's forgotten
it lingers

pretends to look for its appointment in the datebook

but in the end it touches you
and is an
inextricable tar

it leaves no scar

extracts the smallest from the house
invites it
to the icy dance

EL HAMBRE OCURRE

el hambre
su alquimia pertinaz

transmutación violenta
en la costilla

tener un hombre vivo entre los dedos
tirárselo a la muerte

el hambre es una muerte
que se hace la olvidada
se demora

finge buscar su cita en la libreta

pero al final te toca
y es una brea
inarrancable

no deja cicatriz

o sustrae al más pequeño de la casa
lo convida
al baile helado

hunger happens
I'm writing this in Costa Rica
it's September 1985

but it turns out
that death here is catholic and apostolic
the dream in which we dwell doesn't withstand
these shackles
so no one comments
hunger remains a gesture of bad taste

peace

here peace is nourished with blood

translated by Barbara Paschke

el hambre ocurre
esto lo escribo en Costa Rica
estamos en setiembre ochenta y cinco

pero resulta
la muerte aquí es católica apostólica
el sueño en que moramos no resiste
este grillete
así nadie comenta
el hambre queda en rasgo de mal gusto

la paz

aquí la paz se nutre con la sangre

PRECIOUS MAHOGANY

I tried to defend you,
I thought there might be
Someone else who loved you
As I love you.

Here I am, beneath you
Caressing your precious timber,
Protecting you with my hands
From those who claim to love you.

Lies!
They see you bleed and they laugh as they stuff their pockets
With dollars, from your suffering.

translated by Jessica Powell

Editors' note: This poem was originally written in Spanish and then self-translated into Miskito (the poet's mother tongue), displayed here. The English translation is based on the original Spanish.

YULU DUSA PRANAKIRA

Kainam kahbaia trai kaikiri,
Ban kra luki kapri
Upla wala sim bara kan latwan
Yang wina man ra brisna baku.

Nara sana man mununhtamra
Dusa karnika pranakira ra
Mihti wal sapi mai bri sna kainam kahbi
Baha nani latwan wi nani ba wina.

Kunin!
Talim tahwi kan kaiki al lilia sa al pakitka
Nani dalas wal bangkai ba man wiham latwanka wal.

AMANDA CASTRO

HOW DARE THEY SAY

that I am the shit of the world
that I will burn in hell
for loving you
      woman

If those
who boasted the true right to possess you
invented the electric shock
for your belly
kept you pregnant in jail
to sell your child to a rich man
accused you of being mad
because you searched for your child in the plazas
and on the sidewalks.

How dare they say
that God will never have to bless
my union
to this other woman
who never raised a hand to me
who after a thousand men
was the only one to teach me to laugh
"like an animal now freed"

CÓMO SE ATREVEN A DECIR

que soy la mierda del mundo
que se quemará en el infierno
por amarte
       mujer

Si ellos
que decían tener el verdadero derecho de poseerte
inventaron la picana
para tu vientre
te mantuvieron preñada en una cárcel
para vender tu hijo a un hombre rico
te acusaron de estar loca
porque buscabas a tu hijo en las plazas
y en las veredas.

Cómo se atreven a decir
que Dios jamás habrá de bendecir
mi unión
a esa otra mujer
que jamás me levantó una mano
que después de mil hombres
fue la única que me enseñó a reír
"como un animal que ha sido puesto en libertad"

This woman
who is a mirror

We never launched a bomb
    Not in the name of God
    Nor in the name of race
    Nor in the name of patriotism
    And less so
in that of revolution
We
    Hear in the blood
its brutal underground echo

We never said
    "burn those traitors"
nor did we throw the first stone

We
didn't even dare
to scream in their faces
that the world's shit
was born from them
with their "divine truth"

translated by Emily Toder

Esta mujer
que es un espejo

Nosotras jamás lanzamos una bomba
        Ni en el nombre de Dios
        Ni de la raza
        Ni de la patria
        Y menos
de la revolución
Nosotras
        Escuchamos en la sangre
su brutal eco subterráneo

Nosotras nunca dijimos
        "quémenlas por traidoras"
ni arrojamos la primera piedra

Nosotras
ni siquiera nos atrevimos
a gritarles a la cara
que la mierda del mundo
la parieron ellos
con su "verdad divina"

DECRIMINALIZING POEM

You spread your legs

but another slipped in
like a wet
worm and now
he says
your legs are not
your own
your ovaries either
Your body belongs to christ
or to the congress
of the nation
voting on your permission
to occupy it
Nobody
is born alone
and you're not someone else's
milk machine
not the test tube or the dropper
You're not
an incubating object
Mother is not
to birth
Father is not
to fuck

POEMA DESPENALIZADOR

Vos abriste las piernas

pero otro se metió
como una lombriz
mojada y ahora
dice
que tus piernas no son
tuyas
ni tus ovaries
Tu cuerpo es de cristo
o del congreso
de la nación
que vota el permiso
que tenés de habitarlo
Nadie
nace solo
y vos no sos un instrumento
de leche ajena
la probeta o el gotero
Vos no sos
un objeto incubador
Madre no es
parir
Padre no es
cojer

A spermatozoid
is not
a stone
it too is alive
it consumes oxygen
just like mosquitos
in the washbasin
Why don't they put it
up for adoption
give it a name
and a flowery
dress
because a cell
they say
is worth the same
as you

translated by Will Vanderhyden

Un espermatozoide
no es
una piedra
también está vivo
consume oxígeno
igual que los mosquitos
en la palangana
Por qué no lo dan
en adopción
pongámosle un nombre
y un vestido
de flores
porque una célula
dicen
vale lo mismo
que vos

MY NAME

My name,
dried-up hide,
mouth to mouth bitten,
gnashed by the eye-teeth of the people.
I have peeled off the rags from my name
as a serpent slips its skin.
Who dares blaspheme the moon as prostitute?
She is accustomed to stroll with night,
accustomed to wage her body,
accustomed to bury her shame,
accustomed to drown in darkness because she detests her clarity.
Because she is a sublime white vermin.
My name,
The prohibited chew-gum for the tiny ones.
My name,
Stomped on by the all-disdain.
Now I have no name.
I am a crazy caller who tousles love's long tresses.

translated by Juan Felipe Herrera

Editors' note: This poem was originally written in Yucatecan Mayan and was translated into Spanish by the poet. The English translation is based on her Spanish version.

IN K'ABA'

In k'abae,
tikín ot'el,
chi'il chi' u chi'chi'al,
u chá'acha'al tumén u dzay máako'ob.
Dzok in pitik u nóok'il in k'aba'
je bix u podzikúbal kan tu xla sóol.
¿Baanten ma' tan u yala xkakbach ti' uj?
Leti'e suk u xínbal bul ák'ab,
suk u bulik u uínklil,
suk u balik u su'tal,
suk u t'ubkubaj ich ek'jochénil tumén dzok u p'ektik u sáasil.
Tumén leti'e sak kichpán xba'ba'al.
In k'abae,
cha takan ti' páalal.
In k'abae,
tatak'cha'tan tumén p'ek.
Bejlae mina'an in k'aaba.
Tené aluxén tan in sosok'ik u tzotzel u pool yáamaj.

IF, ONE DAY, ON YOUR STREET CORNER, DEATH COMES TO YOU

If, one day, on your street corner, death comes to you as a stray bullet; if death grabs you from behind and kisses you on the back of your neck with its tooth of lead; if death whispers in your ear that it loves you and asks you to come lie down beside it on the sidewalk, would you think of José de Espronceda? Would you say that it is his place not yours? To die like that in the crossfire between drug dealers and cops, to die like that for no reason before getting home with the morning bread, to die like that as others used to die in distant lands, to die like that, like a flower crushed by a tank—you think—it isn't fair. It isn't fair—you repeat—and you keep on walking.

translated by Katherine Silver

SI UN DÍA, EN LA ESQUINA DE TU CALLE, TE ALCANZA LA MUERTE

Si un día, en la esquina de tu calle, te alcanza la muerte como una bala perdida; si la muerte te atrapa por la espalda y te besa en la nuca con su diente de plomo; si la muerte te susurra que te ama y te pide yacer a su lado en medio de la acera, ¿pensarías en José de Espronceda?, ¿dirías que ese es su lugar y no el tuyo? Morir así entre el fuego cruzado del Narco y los Federales, morir así de gratis sin llegar a tu casa con el pan de la mañana, morir así como antes morían otros en tierras lejanas, morir así como una flor aplastada por un tanque de guerra—piensas—no es justo. No es justo—repites—y sigues caminando.

OUR WOVEN HISTORIES

A huipil doesn't speak to you
it recounts your soul,
a huipil doesn't cover you
it embraces your heart,
a huipil doesn't chafe
it caresses your chest,
a huipil doesn't stain you
it tattoos your skin.

A huipil shows you
the years of love and strength
it took to survive,
for us to exist.

A huipil tells you
about the dead rising from the ashes
about shining colors that block out scorn and discrimination
about preserving Mother Nature's body.

The huipil
is a poem made by our ancestors that you embrace
a codex of threads that the invaders could not disappear
it is our culture's memory
it is science, it is art, it is a living calendar.

PERAJ TAQ SIPANÏK

Jun po't man choj ta nich'on chawe'
rija' nusik'ij jun pach'un tzij chi re awanima,
jun po't man choj ta yatruküch
rija' nuq'etej ak'u'x,
jun po't man choj ta yatrupïtz'
rija' numalalej ruwa' ak'u'x,
jun po't man choj ta yatrukïch
rija' nuk'ät nub'onij ach'akul.

Jun po't nuk'üt chawe'
ronojel ri juna' ri ruxak'om pe ri' rik'in ajowab'äl
richin ruk'aslemal
chuqa' richin qak'aslemal.

Jun po't nutzijoj chawe'
achike rub'eyal yataläx pe chi ruxe' ri aq'al richin kamïk
achike rub'eyal ri jeb'ël taq b'onil ri nikiyoj ruwäch ri
     tz'ilanem
achike rub'eyal nichajïx ruch'akul Qate' ruwach'ulew.

Ri po't
re' jun pach'un tzij richin naq'etëj ri xkib'än kan ri ojer
     qawinaq
jun ojer tzib'awuj b'atz' rub'anikil ri man xetikir ta
     xkichüp el ruwäch ri emajonel

When these histories come together
they embroider lives
they embroider knowledge
they embroider generations of spiraling energy,
they braid voices
they braid wisdom
they braid songs
they braid everyday poetry,
they make us fall in love with the poch'on
with the pajon
with the k'ajin
with the kumatzin
with the b'aq'otin . . .

From the moment a huipil is born
beneath the arms of the peach groves
beneath a winking Father Sun
it becomes an important part of the family
deserving love and respect.
Like my great-grandmother said:
"Mija: give thanks to the huipil you are taking care of,
        and when you put it on, ask it to care for you."

translated by Paul Worley

Editors' note: This poem is written in Maya Kaqchikel.

rija' ri nataxik richin qab'anob'al richin qati't qamama'
rija' etamab'alil, rija' na'ojinïk, rija' jun k'äs cholq'ij.

toq nitz'ïs kichi' jun ka'i' peraj
nikitz'ïs k'aslem
nikitz'ïs na'ojil
nikitz'ïs uchuq'ab'il k'aslemal pa setesïk,
nikipach'uj ch'ab'äl
nikipach'uj nima'etamab'äl
nikipach'uj b'ix
nikipach'uj pach'un tzij ri niqab'än jantape',
yojkib'ochi'ij rik'in ri poch'on
rik'in ri pajon
rik'in ri k'ajin
rik'in ri kumatzin
rik'in ri b'aq'otin . . .

Toq jun po't naläx
chi ruxe' ruq'a' taq tra's
chi ruxe' runaq' ruwäch qatata' q'ij
nok jun chik alk'wal richin ri ach'alalri'ïl
ruma ri k'o chi niya' ruq'ij chuqa' ajowab'äl chi re
achi'el xub'ij kan rute' wati't
"Wal: Tak'awomaj chi re apo't ri nayäk kan chuqa'
          tak'utuj chi re ri nawokisaj chi katruchajij."

THE BRIDGE

water tanks wells reservoirs
recently planted trees
amid coal dust and oil-stained trenches
amid the sound of morning   water against pails

though it doesn't exist it's a world
you suspect inhabited and material
every time when in your bed
you are awakened by a sensation of sand

the events of that desert
await their turn
moth-eaten   unstitched   cramped
they form long lines on the Lima Bridge

do not trust the room's familiar things
if you look at the underside of the pillowcase
you will discover that by means of minute particles
the desert tries to transplant
a little bit of kerosene
a little bit of vicious dog

the flag or the stake that gives it a foothold in the city.

translated by Jessica Powell

EL PUENTE

tanques de agua pozos reservorios
árboles recién plantados
entre el polvillo de carbón y zanjas manchadas de aceite
entre el ruido de la mañana   el agua contra los baldes

un mundo que si bien no existe
sospechas poblado y material
cada vez que en la cama
te despierta una sensación de arena

los sucesos de aquel desierto
permanecen a la espera de su turno
apolillados   descosidos   acalambrados
forman largas colas sobre el Puente de Lima

no confíes en lo conocido de la habitación
si examinas el revés de la funda
descubrirás que a través de diminutas partículas
el desierto intenta trasladar
un poco de querosene
un poco de perro bravo

la bandera o la estaca que le permita establecerse en la ciudad.

MARGARITA LOSADA VARGAS

THE WALL

in any case
there will always be an ache
an image
a taste

a poem recalling
that we are children
of a singular dead language

translated by Idra Novey

EL MURO

de todos modos
siempre habrá un dolor
una imagen
un sabor

un poema recordando
que somos hijos
de una única lengua muerta

POISONOUS POETRY

Sorry I don't meet your expectations
The thing is, I'm difficult, I cause consternation
Motivated by the polemic of the stage
No one pulls the curtains, the show's all the rage—
Full house, lights up, a scene in shadows
No one names me but I'm there in the shade
Far from the red spotlight of desire
They're here to see me play a part I don't buy
They clap, they're having the time of their lives
As my tears bring all the suffering to life—
I've been fishing words since I was born
I swallow it all so I can spit out feeling
No one's announced me on any billboard
A few months back I was an ordinary girl
When I looked in the mirror my heart went stone
Listen, my snakes swallowed so much poison ivy

Poisonous poetry, I sweat poisonous poetry
From my pores I sweat poisonous poetry
Nothing makes sense if I say it deliriously
Show's over, shower me with poisoned lilies
Poisonous poetry, I sweat poisonous poetry
From my pores I sweat poisonous poetry
Nothing makes sense if I say it deliriously
Show's over, shower me with poisoned lilies

POESÍA VENENOSA

Lamento mucho no cumplir con sus expectativas
Lo que pasa es que soy un poco conflictiva
Me motiva la polémica de las artes escénicas
Nadie corre el telón y las butacas están llenas
Prende la luz y solo se proyectan sombras
Nadie me nombra pero salgo a la penumbra
Donde no alumbra el foco rojo del deseo
De verme interpretar un personaje que no creo
Cómo disfrutan aplaudiendo
Cuando con mis lágrimas le doy vida a todo el sufrimiento
Pescar palabras lo traigo de nacimiento
Me las trago todas para escupir el sentimiento
No me anunciaron en ninguna cartelera
Hacia unos meses atrás era una muchacha cualquiera
Al verme en el espejo el corazón se me hizo piedra
Es que mis serpientes se tragaron mucha hiedra venenosa

Poesía venenosa, por los poros sudo poesía venenosa
Nada tiene sentido si lo digo en el delirio
Se termina la función regálenme ramos de lirios venenosa
Poesía venenosa, por los poros sudo poesía venenosa
Nada tiene sentido si lo digo en el delirio
Se termina la función regálenme ramos de lirios

Today I want to sing out every wild thing
Postmodern feminist of eternal spring
Trying to live off art, though I don't really want to
I got lost in time, lost track of this age
Not everyone can break a leg onstage
Or wreck her voice with bad acoustics
In guatemala with a shattered soul
They'd sooner bomb me than see me score a goal
To hell with criticisms of how I look
Don't want to smile all the time, I'll keep my bad moods
This low-budget hypocritical performance
Has no moral control, let alone hormonal
I bet you they won't pay for this
They'll criticize 'cause they didn't want this
They wanted to relax, not hear my inner conflict
To handle me they'd better eat poison ivy

Poisonous poetry, I sweat poisonous poetry
From my pores I sweat poisonous poetry
Nothing makes sense if I say it deliriously
Show's over, shower me with poisoned lilies
Poisonous poetry, I sweat poisonous poetry
From my pores I sweat poisonous poetry
Nothing makes sense if I say it deliriously
Show's over, shower me with poisoned lilies
Poisonous
Poisonous poetry

translated by Carolina de Robertis

Hoy tengo ganas de cantar incoherencias
Feminista posmoderna de la eterna primavera
Intento vivir del arte aunque realmente no quiera
Me perdí en el tiempo y me equivoqué de era
No es cualquiera la que se rompe la pierna en las tablas
La que lastima su voz porque la acústica esta mala
En guatemala con el alma astillada
Antes de verme triunfar me tirarán una granada
Para nada agradezco que critiquen mi fachada
No me gusta andar sonriendo porque soy malhumorada
Este hipócrita espectáculo de bajo presupuesto
No tiene control moral ni hormonal por supuesto
Les apuesto que no pagarán por esto
Me criticarán porque no soy lo que quisieron
Querían relajarse no oír mi conflicto interno
Para soportarme deberán comerse hiedra venenosa

Poesía venenosa, por los poros sudo poesía venenosa
Nada tiene sentido si lo digo en el delirio
Se termina la función regálenme ramos de lirios venenosa
Poesía venenosa, por los poros sudo poesía venenosa
Nada tiene sentido si lo digo en el delirio
Se termina la función regálenme ramos de lirios
venenosa
Poesía venenosa

Editors' note: As "Poesía venenosa" is a rap song, we encourage you to listen to an online video or digital download in order to experience the dynamic power of the lyrics' rhythm and spirit when performed by Rebeca.

TO PRESIDENT-ELECT

There's no fence, there's a tunnel, there's a hole in the wall, yes, you think right now ¿no one's running? Then who is it that sweats and shits their shit there for the cactus. We craved water; our piss turned the brightest yellow—I am not the only nine-year-old who has slipped my backpack under the ranchers' fences. I'm still in that van that picked us up from "Devil's Highway." The white van honked three times, honks heard by German shepherds, helicopters, Migra trucks. I don't know where the drybacks are who ran with dogs chasing after them. Correction: I do know. At night, they return to say *sobreviviste bicho, sobreviviste carnal*. Yes, we over-lived.

Editors' note: This poem was written before the 2016 United States presidential election was decided. The poem was originally written in English and then self-translated into Spanish by the author.

CORRIENDO

No hay muro, hay un túnel, un hoyo en la pared, sí,
¿pensás que ahorita nadie está corriendo? Quien es
pues, el que suda y caga su mierda en el cactus.
Añoramos agua; nuestro orín se hizo amarillo-amarillo—yo
no soy el único niño con su mochila debajo de los cercos
de los gringos. Todavía voy en esa van blanca
que nos recogió en el Devil's Highway. La van blanca
pitó tres veces, pero escuchamos a los pastores alemanes,
helicópteros, La Migra. No sé adonde están
los espaldas-secas que corrieron cuando los chuchos
los seguían. Corrección: si sé. Por la noche, regresan
para decirme, sobreviviste bicho, sobreviviste carnal. Pues sí,
sobre-requete-que-vivimos.

ABOUT THE POETS

CARLOS AGUASACO (COLOMBIA, 1975-)

Born in Bogotá, Aguasaco's writing has focused on resistance to narcotrafficking as well as issues surrounding the peace process in his native Colombia. His writing has been included in numerous anthologies and has been featured in a variety of media outlets. He has co-edited six anthologies and authored three poetry collections. Aguasaco is the founder and director of Artepoetica Press, a publishing house specializing in Hispanic American themes and authors. He is also the director of the Americas Poetry Festival of New York. Aguasaco is currently an associate professor of Latin American Cultural Studies and Spanish at the City College of New York.

JOSÉ MARÍA ARGUEDAS (PERU, 1911-1969)

Writer, researcher, and promoter of the Quechuan cultures of the Andes, Arguedas was also a university professor and civil servant. Among the positions he held were director of Peru's Casa de la Cultura and National History Museum. He has been awarded many distinguished prizes for his fiction. His poems in Quechua embrace the spirit of the Andean tradition and the spirit of protest, and highlight the social and ecological realities of his surroundings. After struggling for many years with anxiety and depression, he committed suicide in 1969.

NICOLAS BEHR (BRAZIL, 1958-)

Unable to go to print traditionally due to the Brazilian dictatorship's censorship, Behr's first poetic work, *Iogurte com Farinha* (1977), was printed by mimeograph, passed hand to hand, and became a bestseller. Over thirty more volumes would follow in the subsequent decades. In the 1980s, he made a living writing advertisements, and in 1982, he contributed to the foundation MOVE, Movimento Ecológico de Brasília, the first environmental nongovernmental organization in the capital. In 1986, he left the advertising business to dedicate himself to ecology, particularly to the production of native seedlings. He would continue publishing poetry in the '90s and eventually published his book of poetry *Poesília* (2010), which compiles the author's texts involving the city where he lives, Brasília—a city that appears reformulated as a utopian proposal under the conceptual name of "Braxília."

GIOCONDA BELLI (NICARAGUA, 1948–)

Renowned writer, feminist, and militant Sandinista, Belli was sent into exile in Mexico and Costa Rica because of her opposition to the Nicaraguan dictator Anastasio Somoza. With the triumph of the revolution, she carried out important work in the new government until 1986. Her poetry, considered revolutionary in a political sense as well as feminist and erotic, won important awards such as the Casa de las Américas Prize in 1978 for her book *Linea de Fuego*. Her semi-autobiographical novel, *La mujer habitada*, has been translated into fourteen languages and has sold over a million copies. It won the 1989 Librarians, Editors, and Booksellers Prize for best political novel of the year in Germany. Now an outspoken former member of the Frente Sandinista de Liberación Nacional party, currently in power in Nicaragua, she has been accused of terrorist activities and writes under great political risk. In 2019, she was awarded the Oxfam Novib/PEN International Award for Freedom of

Expression for her commitment to free speech despite the danger to her own life.

MARIO BENEDETTI (URUGUAY, 1920-2009)

A prolific writer, journalist, and member of the Generation '45, Mario Benedetti collaborated on the most influential literary, cultural, and political journals of his native Uruguay, including the weekly paper *Marcha*, of which he also became director. *Marcha* was shut down by the military dictatorship in 1974. His many political and literary activities include founding and directing the Center of Literary Research of the Casa de las Américas, co-founding the leftist-Marxist political party March 26 Movement, and directing the Department of Hispanoamerican Literature at the Universidad de la República in Montevideo. He abandoned this last post to flee the country after the 1973 coup d'état, and did not return for two decades, though he continued to write prolifically while living in exile in various other countries. He has received numerous awards and recognitions, including the Queen Sofía Prize for Ibero-American Poetry (1999) and the Ibero-Americano Prize José Martí (2001).

REI BERROA (DOMINICAN REPUBLIC, 1949-)

Poet, cultural promoter, and literary critic, Berroa is currently the chair of George Mason University's Department of Modern and Classical Languages, where he has taught since 1989, specializing in Latin American literature. He has traveled extensively as a speaker and a poet, participating in numerous international poetry festivals such as the Festival of Izmir, Turkey, in 2008, and the International Poetry Festival in Medellín,

Colombia, in 2010. In 2014, New York City's annual Dominican Book Fair was dedicated to Berroa, and he was honored at Santo Domingo's 2018 International Book Fair. In honor of his lifetime achievements, Berroa has received the Mihai Eminescu Prize (Romania), the Trieste Poesia International Prize, and the Médaille de Vermeil (Paris, France). Since 2001, he has published an anthology of the poets invited to participate in his celebrated "Poetry Marathon," held every year at the Library of Congress and the Teatro de la Luna in Arlington, Virginia.

ERNESTO CARDENAL (NICARAGUA, 1925–2020)

A Catholic priest who was a vanguard of Liberation Theology, Ernesto Cardenal was a famed Sandinista poet, revolutionary, and politician who participated in the 1954 revolution against the military dictatorship of Anastasio Somoza. With the triumph by the Sandinistas in 1979, he filled the position of minister of culture until 1987. He eventually came to criticize the government of the Sandinista Daniel Ortega, and moved his support to the Sandinista Renewal Movement. Among his numerous awards was the prestigious Peace Prize of the German Book Trade in 1980 and the Pablo Neruda Ibero-American Prize for Poetry in 2009. He received honorary doctorates from numerous universities in the United States and Spain, and was nominated for the Nobel Prize in Literature.

ROSARIO CASTELLANOS (MEXICO, 1925–1974)

Castellanos was an influential intellectual, diplomat, writer, and feminist. Beginning with her first writings, she called attention to the discrimination and exploitation to which Indigenous communities were subjected, injustices that she had witnessed growing up on her parents' farm in Chiapas. Castellanos unites the Indigenous cause with the feminist fight for women's rights in numerous emblematic works of theater, essay, poetry, and fiction. Castellanos was a university professor in Mexico and the United States, and served as Mexico's ambassador to Israel, where she was also involved in academia. She received many awards and recognitions, including the Xavier Villaurrutia Prize (1958) and the Sor Juana Inés de la Cruz Prize (1962).

AMANDA CASTRO (HONDURAS, 1962-2010)

After earning a PhD in Latin American Sociolinguistics from the University of Pittsburgh in 1985, Castro lived in the US, teaching at various colleges and universities. She continually fought for women's rights while working to promote the art and literature of female artists and denouncing sexism, gender inequality, and gender violence. The author of several books of poetry, she reveals in her work her passion for feminism and social justice, appealing to a historical rewriting and to a collective consciousness of solidarity. She has defended the rights of sweatshop workers and founded the Siguapate Project to support women's dignity and creativity.

ÓSCAR CERRUTO (BOLIVIA, 1912-1981)

Writer, diplomat, and journalist, Cerruto became initiated in political activism at a young age, a passion that would culminate in the publication of his renowned social novel, *Aluvión de Fuego* (1935), a stark and straightforward portrait of the tumultuous years of social, political, and racial conflict surrounding the Chaco War. The novel effectively placed Cerruto within the movement later known as the Combative Generation. His poetry is infused with his steady preoccupation with social justice, while also standing out for its avant-garde aesthetic and linguistic starkness. Cerruto served as a member of the Bolivian Royal Academy of Language, director of the newspaper *El Diario*, and Bolivian Ambassador to Uruguay, among other posts in public administration.

AIMÉ CÉSAIRE (MARTINIQUE, 1913–2008)

Author and politician Aimé Césaire wrote the influential book *Discours sur le colonialisme*. The volume denounces European colonial and racist oppression, while tackling the concept of Négritude that had recently been coined in the pages of the magazine *L'étudiant noir*, which he had founded in Paris along with other activists and poets, including León-Gontran Damas and Léopold Sédar Senghor. Upon returning to Martinique after his studies in France, he and his wife, the intellectual Suzanne Roussi, founded the magazine *Tropiques*, in which they resisted the stereotyped vision of African culture in their country. With the help of the French Communist Party, Césaire was elected as a representative of the National Assembly and mayor of Fort-de-France, a post that he maintained until 2001. In the 1950s, due to his desire to claim his country's autonomy, he renounced the party and founded the Progressive Martinique Party.

ELICURA CHIHUAILAF (CHILE, 1952–)

One of the most distinguished poets of the Indigenous Mapuche people, Chihuailaf writes in both Spanish and his native language, Mapudungun. His poetic themes include the imagination, Mapuche culture, and criticism of the discrimination to which his people have been and continue to be subjected. He has translated texts by Víctor Jara and Pablo Neruda into Mapudungun, and some of his poems have been set to music by composers, including Eduardo Cáceres. His book *Sueños y Contrasueños* was awarded the Santiago Municipal Prize for Poetry. He has served as the secretary general of the Association of Indigenous Writers.

JUAN GUSTAVO COBO BORDA (COLOMBIA, 1948-)

Diplomat, journalist, and literary critic, Borda has served as subdirector of Colombia's National Library and as cultural secretary of the Republic, among other political and cultural posts. As an author, he is considered a part of the Disenchanted Generation. He has published many collections of poetry and essays and has written frequently on themes of art and literature. He has also published and edited highly influential anthologies of Colombian and South American poetry and has worked as director at the literary magazines *Eco* and *Graceta*. Borda has also served as cultural attaché to Argentina and Spain and as Colombian ambassador to Greece, and he is currently a member of the Colombian Academy of Language.

NEGMA COY (GUATEMALA, 1980-)

Coy is a Maya Kaqchikel writer, painter, actress, and teacher. She writes in Maya Kaqchikel, Spanish, and in Maya glyphs. Her work has drawn international attention and she has been invited to many festivals for both her art and poetry. Coy published six different poetry collections between 2015 and 2019: *XXXK'* (2015); *Soy un búho* (2016); *Lienzos de herencia* (2017); *A orillas del fuego* (2017); *Tz'ula', Guardianes de los caminos* (2019); and *Kikotem—Historias, cuentos y poesía kaq-chikel* (2019). She is active within her community's cooperatives, including Ajtz'ib Escritores de Comalapa, Movimiento de artistas mayas Ruk'u'x, and Arte de Comalapa.

BRICEIDA CUEVAS COB (MEXICO, 1969-)

A Mayan writer who composes and publishes her verses in her native language, Cuevas Cob is a founding member of the Association of Indigenous-Language Writers of Mexico. She has traveled extensively as a conference participant and as a poet, and has instructed important literature workshops in her native region of Calkiní. In 2010, she was selected by the National Fund for Culture and Arts to become a member of the prestigious National System of Art Creators association. Her books include the collection *Ti' u billil in nook'*, published in 2008.

ROQUE DALTON (EL SALVADOR, 1935-1975)

In 1956, Dalton founded the influential University Literary Circle in San Salvador alongside the Guatemalan poet Otto René Castillo. In 1969, he was awarded the prestigious Casa de las Américas Prize for his book of poems *Taberna y otros lugares*. He was part of the literary group called the "Generación Comprometida" (the Committed Generation). His political activism, poetry, and essays led to his repeated imprisonment, during which he escaped execution on two occasions. Dalton later joined the guerrilla force of the People's Revolutionary Army and was eventually assassinated by his own comrades due to an accusation that he had collaborated with the CIA (the accusation was later dismissed as completely false).

LÉON-GONTRAN DAMAS (FRENCH GUIANA, 1912-1978)

In 1934, Léon-Gontran Damas founded the student paper *L'Étudiant noir* along with Aimé Césaire and Léopold Sédar Senghor, which is considered the basis of what would be called the Négritude Movement. Damas was a soldier during the Second World War and later a representative of Guiana in the National Assembly of France, as well as a representative of UNESCO. He traveled to numerous countries as a professor and lecturer. His last post was serving as professor and director of the African Studies Program at Howard University in Washington, DC. His acclaimed book of poems, *Pigments* (1937), has been considered central to the Négritude Movement. When poems from *Pigments* (translated into Baoulé) were recited by African draft resisters in the Ivory Coast in 1939, the book was banned throughout French West Africa.

JULIA DE BURGOS (PUERTO RICO, 1914-1953)

Poet, feminist, and activist, Julia de Burgos was a tremendous civil rights advocate for women and Afro-Caribbeans. She was an active member of the Puerto Rican Nationalist Party, which fought for the independence of the country. Born of humble origins, de Burgos worked a variety of jobs, including as a teacher and later as a journalist for the progressive New York newspaper *Pueblos Hispanos*. When she died in New York, her identity was unknown until the body was claimed by friends and relatives and moved to her birthplace, Carolina, Puerto Rico. Her legacy has inspired many distinguished homages and recognitions, both in her country and in the US.

RENÉ DEPESTRE (HAITI, 1926-)

A writer of communist convictions, Depestre participated in the student uprisings of January 1943, a youthful act for which he was arrested and later exiled. In France, he contacted surrealist and Négritude groups in addition to actively participating in French decolonization movements. His participation in these movements led to his expulsion from the country. Invited by Che Guevara in 1959, Depestre lived in Cuba for an important part of his exile, where he undertook various cultural and governmental posts and founded the famous cultural and writing center the Casa de las Américas. Disillusioned with Castro's regime, he returned to France in 1978, where he worked for UNESCO in Paris. His work has been published in countries around the world and his poetry has appeared in many French, Spanish, and German anthologies and collections. He has spent many years in France, and was awarded the Prix Renaudot in 1988 for his work *Hadriana dans Tous mes Rêves*. He lives in Lézignan-Corbières in southern France and is a special envoy of UNESCO for Haiti.

CARLOS DRUMMOND DE ANDRADE (BRAZIL, 1902-1987)

Carlos Drummond de Andrade is considered one of the most influential Brazilian modernist poets. In addition to being a prolific poet, he is also a translator of literary works by de Balzac, Maeterlink, Molière, and Knut Hamson. Drummond de Andrade was also a journalist, and he filled a variety of government positions, including director of the Património Histórico e Artístico Nacional. His literary work is characterized by its decidedly humanistic nature and a strong commitment to solidarity. In 1983, he declined an important award because it was given by the Brazilian military dictatorship. His work has received many significant awards, and he was considered for the Nobel Prize in Literature.

LOURDES ESPÍNOLA (PARAGUAY, 1954–)

Lourdes Espínola is a diplomat, cultural promoter, writer, and literary critic. She has published numerous volumes of poetry and has received a variety of prestigious awards, including the Hérib Campos Cervera National Poetry Prize (2012), and the Knight of the Ordre des Arts et des Lettres (2011), bestowed on her by the French government. Espínola has traveled internationally as a poet and scholar. She is a full professor at the Universidad Americana and at the Universidad del Norte, and the director of cultural relations and tourism at the Ministry of Foreign Affairs of the Republic of Paraguay.

TERESA CABRERA ESPINOZA (PERU, 1981–)

Teresa Cabrera Espinoza is a poet, essayist, and cultural activist, and is a member of the workshop Taller de Artesanía Salvaje, which focuses on bringing collective research, video art, and political activism into public spaces. She has worked as editor of the magazine *Poder* and has published two acclaimed books of poems, *Sueño de pez o neblina* and *El Nudo*.

CONCEIÇÃO EVARISTO (BRAZIL, 1946–)

Conceição Evaristo is a Brazilian author and scholar of humble origins whose body of work addresses the conditions of marginalized sectors of Brazilian society, denouncing violence and racism but also giving value and voice to those routinely discriminated against, most particularly Black women. She has worked with the Quilombhoje Group since it was founded in the 1980s to promote Afro-Brazilian literature.

KYRA GALVÁN (MEXICO, 1956–)

A prolific writer, Galván has won many prestigious awards and honors for her poetry, including the 1980 Mexican National Young Poet's Prize for her collection *Un pequeño moretón en la piel de nadie*. She has been a fellow at the National Institute of Fine Arts as well as at the Mexican Writers' Center. The feminist perspective in her poems also informs her first novel, *Los indecibles pecados de Sor Juana*, published in 2010.

FERNANDA GARCÍA LAO (ARGENTINA, 1966–)

Fernanda García Lao is a novelist, poet, and playwright. Born in 1966, both of her parents worked as left wing journalists, and in 1975 they were forced to flee to Spain, where they lived in exile for nearly twenty years. When she returned to Argentina in the early '90s, she trained as an actress, playwright, and director. In 1999, her first play, *El sol en la cara*, debuted. Over the next five years, she wrote four more plays, several of which she also acted in and/or directed. Her first novel, *Muerta de hambre*, won the Premio de Novela por el Fondo Nacional de las Artes. She was named "one of the best kept secrets of Latin American Literature" at the 2011 Guadalajara International Book Fair. Her novels, stories, and poems have received wide acclaim, and won various awards and accolades. They have been published in Latin America, Spain, France, Italy, the United States, and Canada.

NICOLÁS GUILLÉN (CUBA, 1902-1989)

Militant communist and staunch defender of the rights of the marginalized, Guillén is considered one of the pioneers of Afro-Antillean poetry. In *Motivos del Son* and *Sóngoro Cosongo, Poemas mulatos* he introduces the son of Cuban music and Afro-Cuban folklore into a literary context, never ceasing to condemn the discrepancies of class and imperialism. He traveled to give speeches and lectures in various countries both before and during his exile from the military regime of Fulgencio Batista. He returned to Cuba during Fidel Castro's revolution. He remained actively involved in the revolution's government until his death, primarily serving as the president of the Union of Writers and Artists of Cuba. Among the many prizes that he has been awarded are the Lenin Peace Prize and the National Prize for Literature.

ANA ISTARÚ (COSTA RICA, 1960-)

Renowned playwright, actress, and poet Istarú's theater work has earned important awards such as the María Teresa de León Prize for drama writers in 1995, and the National Prize for Best Leading Actress in her country in 1997. She received a Guggenheim Fellowship for her artistic work in 1990. Her book of poems *La Estación de fiebre* received the EDUCA Latin American Prize in 1982. Her poetry is sensual and erotic and imbued with a fundamental social commitment to the realities of her country and of Latin America.

VÍCTOR JARA (CHILE, 1932-1973)

Víctor Jara was a legendary, highly influential singer-songwriter of humble, campesino peasant origin. He was also a talented, energetic theater director, focusing on staging Chilean plays.

Jara became famous as a fervent defender of the people through the neofolkloric lyrics of his songs, which unreservedly denounced the abuses of government, war, and authoritarianism, and brought attention to the plight of the workers and those living in poverty. He directed a tribute to Pablo Neruda after the poet won the Nobel Prize, and he vigorously participated in the electoral campaign that would bring Salvador Allende to victory. After Augusto Pinochet's coup d'état in 1973, Jara was arrested along with hundreds of students, employees, and professors of the Universidad Técnica del Estado and was detained with them in the country's major stadium, Estadio Chile, where he was brutally tortured and eventually killed. It was during his imprisonment there that he wrote the poem "Estadio Chile," which a friend hid in his shoe and, after he was released, delivered to Jara's wife. The poem quickly spread around the world. Thirty years after his death, the Estadio Chile was renamed the Estadio Víctor Jara in homage to him and to those who suffered as he did.

RAQUEL JODOROWSKY (CHILE/PERU, 1927-2011)

A prolific poet and painter based in Peru, Jodorowsky came from a family of Ukrainian Jews who sought refuge in Chile, and was born in a copper mine in the country's desert north. She is considered a member of the Generation of '50. In 2008, the Writers Commission of the International Pen Club of Peru honored her for her valiant literary contributions to the country that sheltered her. Similar honors were given at the XIII International Book Fair of Lima. Her books of poetry include *América en la tierra* (1989), *Nazca nacer* (1992), and *Chan-Chan maga lunar* (1992).

REBECA LANE (GUATEMALA, 1984-)

Born Rebeca Eunice Vargas in Guatemala City in the middle of a civil war, she was named after an aunt who had been kidnapped and disappeared by the military government in 1981. As a teenager she became involved with various social movements and with groups of women using art as a means of political expression. Informed by these experiences, she began her own career as a poet and rapper, and, as a self-defined rap feminist and anarchist, has taken her message to international audiences. Her rap lyrics are about her experience in a female body and the struggle of women against sexism. She also speaks out about social problems in Guatemalan society, such as the consequences of war and the lack of justice. In 2014, she won first place in the "Proyecto L" contest with her song "Cumbia de la Memoria," in which she discusses the genocide perpetrated by the military government during the war. She is also a founder of Somos Guerreras (We Are Warriors), a project that strives to transform the hip-hop culture by empowering women.

MARGARITA LOSADA VARGAS (COLOMBIA, 1983-)

Losada Vargas is a poet, psychologist, university professor, and singer in a punk rock band. She is the author of the poetry collections *Mejor Arder* (2013) and *Impermanencia* (2019), and coauthor of *La Persistencia de lo Inútil* (2016). Her work is included in the French-Spanish bilingual anthology of Colombian poetry *Vientre de luz / Ventre de lumiere 14 poetas colombianas + Jattin* (Ladrones del tiempo, 2017), as well as in an Italian anthology, *Il corpo Il eros* (Ladolfi editore, 2018). Losada Vargas also runs the dynamic website www.lugarpoem.com that shares distinctive poety from around the world.

GLAUCO MATTOSO (BRAZIL, 1951-)

The name Glauco Mattoso, which is the pseudonym of the São Paulo writer and countercultural columnist Pedro José Ferreira da Silva, refers to the author's blindness caused by his progressive glaucoma. Like Nicolas Behr, he was part of the generation of underground *poetas marginais* of the 1970s who came together against Brazil's military dictatorship. "Romeu e eu" was first printed in a fanzine, and not published in a book until 1982. During this time, Mattoso participated in the founding of the first gay tabloid and gay group organized in the country. Because of his blindness, he abandoned the graphic side of his poetry in 1995. He dedicated himself primarily to becoming a sonnet writer, publishing more than fifty books in this genre. Mattoso returned to visual and experimental elements as the internet evolved. He also translated Latin American authors into Portuguese, including Jorge Luis Borges and Severo Sarduy.

GABRIELA MISTRAL (CHILE, 1889-1957)

Of humble origins, Gabriela Mistral, literary pseudonym for Lucila Godoy Alcayaga, achieved great success as a grammar-school teacher, pedagogue, essayist, diplomat, and poet. In 1914, while she was working alongside the Mexican Minister of Education José Vasconcelos, her *Sonetos de la muerte* won an important prize at the Floral Games poetry competition in Santiago, Chile, catapulting her career as an author. A tireless traveler, she served in a diverse range of diplomatic posts and spoke at conferences in numerous countries. In 1945, she won the Nobel Prize in Literature, the first ever awarded to a Latin American. Through her poetry and other writing and speeches, she fought against injustices facing children, women, workers, war victims, and Jews. She promoted the identity and independence of Latin America and its Indigenous people. Mistral died in New York. All the royalties from her publications were willed to the poor children of Montegrande, in Chile's Valle del Elqui, where her remains are buried.

NANCY MOREJÓN (CUBA, 1944-)

A distinguished translator and writer, Morejón has won several important awards for her essays and poems, such as the National Essay Prize in 1980 and the National Literature Prize in 2001. Morejón has traveled extensively and has received international acclaim for her work, receiving prestigious recognitions such as the French Republic's National Order of Merit and the Golden Wreath at the annual international poetry festival held in Struga, Macedonia. A significant portion of her work emphasizes Afro-Cuban identity, as well as the role of women in the formation of her nation, seen through a lens of historic reconstruction through the Cuban Revolution, which she supported.

PABLO NERUDA (CHILE, 1904-1973)

Pablo Neruda was born Ricardo Eliecer Neftalí Reyes Basoalto, and grew up in Southern Chile. At sixteen, he took up his pen name and, when he moved to Santiago to study at the University of Chile, he was quickly proclaimed the voice of the radical student movement. At the age of nineteen, he published *Veinte poemas de amor y una canción desesperada*, which would eventually become one of the world's most popular books of poetry. From 1927 to 1932, Neruda served as a consul in East Asia, a period of isolation and depression that fostered the surrealistic verse of his landmark *Residencia en la tierra*. In 1934, he was named consul to Spain, and his experience of the Spanish Civil War changed his poetry, compelling him to write in the more direct style characteristic of resistance poetry. In 1945, he was elected senator as a member of the Chilean Communist Party. While in that role, he denounced his president's oppression of workers and leftists. His arrest was ordered and he fled in exile to Europe. In 1950, he published one of his greatest works, *Canto General*, a Marxist and humanistic interpretation of the history of the Americas. Neruda was named the Chilean Communist Party's candidate for the 1970 presidential elections, but withdrew to support the Socialist-Marxist Salvador Allende. In 1971, while serving as Allende's ambassador to France, Neruda was awarded the Nobel Prize. In 1973, he died twelve days after Augusto Pinochet's military coup, sick from prostate cancer. Two days later, hundreds defied the regime to mourn their poet, filling the streets of Santiago as his funeral became the first public act of resistance against the dictatorship.

JOSÉ EMILIO PACHECO (MEXICO, 1939–2014)

Essayist, poet, translator, novelist, and literary critic, Pacheco was a noted intellectual and member of the Spanish literary movement known as the Generation of '50. His work highlights the refinement of language and social commitment as well as autocriticism, ideas that led him to rewrite some of his own works. Considered one of the most important Mexican poets of the second half of the twentieth century, Pacheco created a varied and influential body of work, which includes eighteen volumes of poetry and many other novels and short stories, that earned him several noteworthy prizes throughout his literary career, including the Mexican National Poetry Prize and the Miguel de Cervantes Prize.

ERNEST PÉPIN (GUADELOUPE, 1950-)

The work of Ernest Pépin, a decorated essayist, narrator, and poet, highlights the Creole movement and culture of his country, both of which centered around values of African origin, orality, and a genuinely Creole Caribbean identity. Before establishing himself as a writer, Pépin was a French professor, a consultant for UNESCO, and the adjunct director of the General Council of Guadeloupe, among other relevant positions. In 2001, he was named director of cultural topics at the General Council of Guadeloupe. Among his many awards are the 1990 Premio Casa de las Américas for his book of poetry *Boucans de mots libres*, for which he also received the Prix Littéraire des Caraïbes in 1993.

BERTALICIA PERALTA (PANAMA, 1939-)

Teacher, journalist, and radio and television scriptwriter, Peralta founded and co-edited the magazine *El Pez Original* (1968–70) and has worked as a theater, music, and literary critic. Her poetry and stories have received various prizes and honorable mentions, such as the José Martí International Conference of Poetry Prize, awarded for her work *Un Lugar en la Esfera Celeste* (1971). In the category of short story, she was twice awarded the National Institute of Culture Prize (1974 and 1980).

JUAN MANUEL ROCA (COLOMBIA, 1946-)

Roca is considered a part of the Disenchanted Generation, which arose after the Colombian neo-avant-garde Nadaístas movement (derived from the Spanish word "nada," meaning "nothing"). Roca's prolific career as a poet, writer, and journalist has won him many prestigious awards and distinctions, among them the Simón Bolívar Prize for Journalism in 1993, the National Poetry Prize for his collection *La hipótesis de nadie* in 2004, and the Casa de las Américas Award for the collection *Biblia de pobres* in 2009. For over a decade, he oversaw the highly influential Magazín Dominical section of the newspaper *El Espectador*. Roca currently teaches writing workshops at the Silva House of Poetry in Bogotá.

ANA MARÍA RODAS (GUATEMALA, 1937–)

Distinguished poet, writer, and journalist Rodas's work has been honored with many prestigious awards. In 1990, she was awarded first prize in two categories—poetry and short story—in the Certamen de Juegos Florales of Mexico, Central America, and the Caribbean. In 2000, she received the Miguel Angel Asturias National Literary Prize. For her journalism, she received the Freedom of the Press Award in 1974. Her first book of poetry, *Poemas de la izquierda erótica* (1973), stands out in particular as a work that both created controversy and garnered international critical recognition.

REINA MARÍA RODRÍGUEZ (CUBA, 1952–)

Author of numerous editions of poetry and prose, including *Luciérnagas* (2017) and *Poemas de Navidad* (2018), Rodríguez won the 1984 Casa de las Américas prize for poetry with *Para un cordero blanco*, followed by the 1998 prize for *La foto del invernadero*. Among her many other awards are the Chevalier medallion of the Ordre des Arts et des Lettres (1999), the

2002 Alejo Carpentier Medal for achievement in Cuban literature, Cuba's 2013 National Prize for Literature, and the Pablo Neruda Ibero-American Prize for Poetry in 2014. Her latest editions in English translation are *Other Letters to Milena* (U. of Alabama Press, 2016) and *The Winter Garden Photograph* (Ugly Duckling Presse, 2019).

JOSÉ LEONEL RUGAMA (NICARAGUA, 1949–1970)

From humble origins, in great measure self-taught, Rugama joined the Sandinista National Liberation Front in 1967. Three years later he died in combat against Somoza's National Guard. His poems had a notable impact both inside and outside of his country, first being published by the university magazine *Taller*. His resistance up until his death at just twenty-one years old embodied the heroic image of a young guerrilla; he stood out as one of the most influential figures of his generation.

NICOMEDES SANTA CRUZ (PERU, 1925–1992)

A distinguished representative and promoter of Afro-Peruvian culture, Nicomedes Santa Cruz traveled to numerous countries primarily as a "decimero," a twentieth-century equivalent of a bard who recites ten-line poems, or "décimas." As he traveled, Santa Cruz also disseminated Afro-Peruvian and Afro-Latin American folklore through journalism, theater, television, music, and radio. He directed the first Festival of Black Art in Cañete, on the central Peruvian coast, collaborated on the conference Négritude and Latin America in Dakar, Senegal, and taught a seminar on African culture in the Dominican Republic. He died in Madrid, where he worked for Spain's public Radio Exterior (Foreign Radio). Due to his work's vindication of Afro-Peruvian historic and cultural value, June 4th, Santa Cruz's birthday, is now celebrated in Peru as the National Day of Afro-Peruvian Culture.

PEDRO SHIMOSE (BOLIVIA, 1940-)

Journalist, professor, essayist, and popular music composer Shimose's volume of poetry *Quiero escribir, pero me sale espuma* won the Casa de las Américas Prize in 1972. Shimose has directed the cultural magazine *Reunión*, and won the Bolivian National Cultural Prize in 1999. He belongs to the Bolivian Academy of Language. Shimose currently lives in Madrid, Spain, where he is part of the Spanish Association of Arts Critics. He also works as a publications advisor for the Ibero-American Cooperation Institute, directing their poetry collection.

MIGUEL OTERO SILVA (VENEZUELA, 1908-1985)

A Marxist writer and journalist, Silva was among the group of university students known as the Generation of '28 that staged acts of resistance to the military regime, events he illustrates in his novel *Fiebre* (1939). Silva's activities and publications led to constant tensions with the series of authoritarian regimes that ruled Venezuela, and he was twice exiled. Following the 1958 fall of the dictatorship of Marcos Pérez Jiménez, under whose administration he had been incarcerated, Silva was elected to the Senate and later went on to found the National Institute of Fine Arts and Culture. Years earlier, he started the influential periodical *El Nacional*. His work is greatly informed by his social, political, and humanitarian commitment, but his humor also stands out, as well as his use of *Costumbrismo*, a Romantic realist literary style focused on documenting the actual nuances of the current culture and happenings.

ROBERTO SOSA (HONDURAS, 1930-2011)

The national poet of Honduras, Roberto Sosa was born in Yoro, where it rains fish once a year. Because of the social and political criticism expressed in his poetry, he came to be considered a "highly dangerous" person by the government, yet he still managed to win important awards, such as the Premio Adonáis de España in 1968, and the Premio Casa de las Américas in 1971. He was in the US many times, first as a master's student at the University of Cincinnati, and then later as a lecturer, writer, and professor of literature. A collaborator and director of influential Honduran and Central American newspapers and magazines, he was decorated as a Knight of the Ordre des Arts et des Lettres in 1990.

ALFONSINA STORNI (ARGENTINA, 1892-1938)

A leading feminist activist, Storni wrote hauntingly beautiful, often erotic poetry that had an international impact. She was born in Switzerland, where her parents were originally from. When she was four, they moved back to Argentina. She worked first as an actress in a traveling theater company and then as a teacher. Later, she held various jobs in Buenos Aires and her poetry eventually had a considerable impact, both nationally and internationally. Despite the obstacles she experienced as a woman, a feminist writer, and a single mother in that time, she succeeded in becoming part of the literary circles made up of the most renowned poets of the period. However, at the height of her career, she was diagnosed with breast cancer. Her body crushed with pain, depressed, and exhausted, Storni walked down a Mar del Plata pier and drowned herself.

CÉSAR VALLEJO (PERU, 1892-1938)

Poet, narrator, playwright, journalist, and political activist César Vallejo's 1922 book, *Trilce*, is considered an essential breakthrough work for the Latin American *Vanguardia* movement. Vallejo lived in Paris, where he collaborated with many European and Latin American intellectuals of the era, including Tristan Tzara, Juan Larrea, and Pablo Neruda. In Spain, he witnessed the rise of the Second Republic and struck up a friendship with writers like Federico García Lorca and Rafael Alberti. He participated in the historic Second International Congress of Antifascist Writers in Valencia in 1937. The horrors of the Spanish Civil War led to the creation of two of his last but most notable works, the book of poetry *España, aparte de mí este cáliz* and the play *La piedra cansada*, both of which were published posthumously. Vallejo died in Paris and is buried in the Cemetery of Montparnasse.

RAQUEL VERDESOTO DE ROMO DÁVILA (ECUADOR, 1910-1999)

A pioneering woman academic of her country, Verdesoto de Romo Dávila was named honorary professor of the Universidad Central de Ecuador. She was a co-founder of the socialist associations Feminine Alliance and Women of Ecuador. She traveled throughout Latin America as a representative of her country and a visiting lecturer, and was a delegate of the National Union of Ecuadorian Educators in Montevideo in 1950. As a researcher and a teacher, Verdesoto de Romo Dávila published scholarly texts, essays, and anthologies of Ecuadorian poetry. Her poetry and essays have received numerous awards and recognitions, such as the Juan León Mera Distinction for her contributions to Ecuadorian literature.

IDEA VILARIÑO (URUGUAY, 1920-2009)

A member of the iconic Generation of '45, Vilariño served as chair of the Uruguayan Literature Department at the University of the Republic in Montevideo, once democracy was restored after the fall of the dictatorship. Vilariño contributed to some of the country's most influential literary magazines, among them *Marcha* and *La Opinión*, and also co-founded other journals, such as *Número*, which she directed. She was a well-respected and award-winning poet, translator (her translations of Shakespeare have been produced in Montevideo), literary critic, cultural researcher, and songwriter of emblematic songs, among them "A una paloma" and "La canción y el poema."

BRIGITTE ZACARÍAS WATSON (NICARAGUA, 1961-)

Brigitte Zacarías Watson is a writer born in Bilwi (Puerto Cabezas), a village on the Atlantic coast of Nicaragua, where ethnicities and languages of a variety of origins—Indigenous (Rama, Sumo-Mayangna, Miskito), African (Creole, Garifuna), and mestizo—all coexist. Due to her schooling in Spanish, Zacarías Watson writes her poetry first in Spanish and then in her native language, Miskito, spoken by at least 150,000 people, primarily along Nicaragua's Caribbean coast. She has served as a social worker for the government of the Nicaraguan North Atlantic Autonomous Region, and has worked for the Nicaraguan Institute of Women.

DAISY ZAMORA (NICARAGUA, 1950-)

An influential author and political activist, Zamora joined the Sandinista National Liberation Front in Nicaragua in 1973, clandestinely acting as programming director and announcer on Radio Sandino. With the triumph of the Sandinista revolution, she took on the responsibilities of vice minister of culture until 1982. Zamora has also been an editor, translator, lecturer, and cultural promoter, particularly of poetry written by women. Her poetic style is marked by its political, humanitarian, and feminist commitments, and she has received important recognition for her work, including a fellowship from the California Arts Council in 2002 and the Mariano Fiallos Gil National Prize for Poetry from the University of Nicaragua in 1977. She currently teaches in San Francisco State University's Department of Latina/Latino Studies.

JAVIER ZAMORA (EL SALVADOR, 1990-)

Javier Zamora's father fled El Salvador when Javier was a year old, as did his mother when he was about to turn five. Both parents' migrations were caused by the US-funded Salvadoran Civil War (1980–1992). In 1999, Zamora migrated through Guatemala, Mexico, and eventually the Sonoran Desert. After a coyote abandoned his group in Oaxaca, Zamora managed to make it to Arizona with the aid of other migrants. His first full-length collection, *Unaccompanied* (Copper Canyon Press, 2017), explores how immigration and the civil war have impacted his family. Zamora graduated from Cal-Berkeley, was a 2018–2019 Radcliffe Fellow at Harvard University, and holds fellowships from CantoMundo, Colgate University (Olive B. O'Connor), MacDowell, Macondo, the National Endowment for the Arts, Poetry Foundation (Ruth Lilly), Stanford University (Stegner), and Yaddo. Zamora was also the recipient of a 2017 Lannan Literary Fellowship, the 2017 Narrative Prize, and the 2016

Barnes & Noble Writers for Writers Award for his work on the Undocupoets Campaign. Zamora lives in Harlem, New York, and is working on a memoir and his second collection of poems, which addresses the current immigration crisis.

RAÚL ZURITA (CHILE, 1950-)

The Poetry Foundation has described Raúl Zurita as "one of Latin America's most celebrated and controversial poets." Poet, performer, professor, and activist, Raúl Zurita conceives of poetry as a total art that intervenes and integrates into a variety of spaces beyond the page, such as lines of verse written from the white smoke of five small planes in the sky above New York City, or the words "Neither pain nor fear" written throughout the Chilean desert. Zurita's poetry expresses and denounces the violence and atrocities committed against the Chilean people by the Pinochet dictatorship. He himself was arrested on the morning of the military coup, September 11, 1973, then detained and tortured on an overcrowded cargo boat, an infamous "prison ship," for six weeks. Later, Zurita also co-founded the artists' action group Colectivo de Acción de Arte, CADA, in protest of the Pinochet regime. In condemnation of the Pinochet regime, Zurita attempted to burn his eyes with ammonium acid, not wanting to further witness the suffering surrounding him (though the attempt to blind himself failed). Among his many recognitions, Zurita won a 1984 Guggenheim Fellowship, the 2000 National Poetry Prize of Chile, and the 2006 Casa de la Américas Prize (for his book *INRI*).

ABOUT THE EDITORS

MARK EISNER has spent most of the past two decades working on projects related to Pablo Neruda. In 2018, Ecco published his *Neruda: The Biography of a Poet* (in hardcover as *The Poet's Calling*), named a finalist for the PEN/Bograd Weld Prize for Biography. Eisner also conceived of, edited, and was one of the principal translators for City Lights' *The Essential Neruda: Selected Poems* (2004). He also wrote the introduction to City Lights' first-ever English translation of Neruda's *venture of the infinite man* (2017). He is now developing a documentary on Neruda. An initial version, narrated by Isabel Allende, won the Latin American Studies Association Award of Merit in Film. Eisner was also involved in the early stages of the Red Poppy Art House in San Francisco, and continues to lead Red Poppy, a literary nonprofit focused on Latin American poetry (www.redpoppy.net). He is currently at work on a new book about the revolutionary photographer Tina Modotti's life and work in Mexico during the 1920s.

In 1995, Eisner earned a BA with distinction in political science with a focus on Latin America, and high honors in English/Creative Writing from the University of Michigan. In 2000, he received a fellowship to pursue an MA degree from Stanford University in Latin American Studies, where he subsequently served as a research fellow and then as a visiting scholar.

He contributed several new translations to *Resistencia*. Find out more about Eisner's work at www.markeisner.net.

TINA ESCAJA is a Spanish American author, digital artist, and Distinguished Professor of Romance Languages and Gender and Women's Studies at the University of Vermont. As a literary critic, she has published extensively on gender and contemporary Latin American and Spanish poetry and technology. Considered a pioneer in electronic literature, Escaja's creative work transcends the traditional book format, leaping into digital art, robotics, augmented reality, and multimedia projects exhibited in museums and galleries internationally. Her collection of poems, *Manual Destructivista / Destructivist Manual* (2016), with translations from the original Spanish by Kristin Dykstra, was selected among the top ten bilingual readings chosen by the *Latino Poetry Review* in 2017. Among other recognitions and awards, she received in 2003 the Dulce María Loynaz International Poetry Prize for her collection *Caída Libre*. In 2015, Fomite Press published a bilingual edition of the collection, translated by Mark Eisner (co-editor of this anthology). Escaja's poems, fiction, and digital work have appeared in numerous anthologies and have been translated into six languages. She is the instigator of the Destructivist/a Movement, initiated on the grave of Vicente Huidobro in October of 2014, and she travels around the world performing Destructivist/a happenings. Escaja has also served as vice president and president of international organizations, such as the Asociación de Estudios de Género y Sexualides (Association of Gender and Sexualities Studies); Feministas Unidas, Inc.; and ALDEEU (Association of Spanish Professionals in the Americas), and is currently a corresponding member of ANLE (American Academy of the Spanish Language) and vice president of Red Poppy. A selection of Escaja's literary and digital projects can be experienced at www.tinaescaja.com.

ABOUT THE TRANSLATORS

JACK AGÜEROS was a Puerto Rican poet, community activist, and translator. Born in New York City, he served a crucial role in promoting the inclusion of Puerto Rican artists in the American art world. He directed the influential El Museo del Barrio in East Harlem from 1977 to 1986. He eventually guided it "to embody the culture of all of Latin America." In 1979, he co-founded the annual Museum Mile Festival on Fifth Avenue. Agüeros published many poems and translations, which were frequently anthologized, and was the author of three books of poetry: *Lord, Is This a Psalm?* (2002), *Sonnets from the Puerto Rican* (1996), and *Correspondence Between the Stone Haulers* (1991), all published by Hanging Loose Press. His collection of Julia de Burgos translations, *Songs of the Simple Truth*, was published by Cornerstone in 1997. In 2012, Agüeros received the Asan World Prize for Poetry.

JEAN ANDREWS is an associate professor in Hispanic Studies at the University of Nottingham, UK. She has written academic articles on several women poets and is presently engaged in an academic study of women's poetry in Spain and Portugal in the years 1936–1975. She edited the Spanish Civil War poetry of Carmen Conde, *Mientras los hombres mueren* (Manchester University Press), and translated it for a separate publication, *While the Men Are Dying* (Arima). She translated the late eighteenth-century *Lament of Eileen O'Connell* from Gaelic in *Sí-Orphans of the Plaintive Air* (Arima) and is currently working on a translation of the work of the forgotten Portuguese mid-twentieth-century poet Maria Valupi. She has published five volumes of her own poetry. Working with Nancy Morejón on "Black Woman" was her first foray into poetry translation proper and she is forever grateful to Nancy for her kindness.

HÉLÈNE CARDONA is a poet, translator, and actor, the recipient of over twenty honors and awards, including the Best Book and International Book Awards, Naji Naaman Literary Prize, Hemingway Grant, and fellowships from the Goethe-Institut and Andalucía International University. She has authored three collections: *Life in Suspension, Dreaming My Animal Selves, The Astonished Universe,* and four translations: José Manuel Cardona's *Birnam Wood,* Gabriel Arnou-Laujeac's *Beyond Elsewhere,* Dorianne Laux's *Ce que nous portons,* Walt Whitman's *Civil War Writings* for WhitmanWeb. Her work has been translated into sixteen languages. Fluent in six languages, she holds an MA in American Literature from the Sorbonne, worked as a translator/interpreter for the Canadian Embassy, and taught at Hamilton College and LMU. Acting credits include *Chocolat, Ford v. Ferrari, Star Trek: Discovery, The Romanoffs, The Hundred-Foot Journey, Dawn of the Planet of the Apes, Happy Feet 2,* and *Serendipity,* among many others. She coproduced the award-winning documentary *Femme.*

MEGAN COXE is a translator and writer whose work has appeared in the *Bitter Oleander, Poetry Quarterly,* and the *End of Austin,* among other publications. She has a masters in Hispanic Literatures from the University of Texas at Austin and has continued to engage with Latin American creative traditions through her fiction and translation work. Most recently, her translations were included in the 2018 biography by Mark Eisner, *Neruda: The Biography of a Poet.*

ANNA DEENY MORALES is a dramatist, translator of poetry, and literary critic. Recent adaptations of Spanish *zarzuelas* include *Cecilia Valdés* (2018) and *La Paloma at the Wall* (2019), both commissioned by the In Series and performed at Gala Hispanic Theater. Her one-act opera libretto, *¡ZAVALA-ZAVALA!: an opera in v cuts*, commissioned by the University of North Carolina, Charlotte, and composer Brian Arreola, will debut in 2021. A 2018 National Endowment for the Arts fellowship recipient for the translation of *Tala* by Gabriela Mistral, Deeny Morales has translated poetry by Raúl Zurita, Mercedes Roffé, Amanda Berenguer, Malú Urriola, Nicanor Parra, and Marosa di Giorgio, among others. Her translation of Alejandra Pizarnik's *Diana's Tree* was published by Shearsman Books in 2020. She received a PhD from the University of California, Berkeley, and teaches at Georgetown University. Her book manuscript, *Other Solitudes*, considers trans-American dialogues on consciousness and poetry.

CAROLINA DE ROBERTIS, a writer of Uruguayan origins, is the author of four novels, most recently *Cantoras*, which received a Stonewall Book Award and a Reading Women Award, and was a Kirkus Prize finalist and a *New York Times* Editors' Choice. Her books have been translated into seventeen languages and have received numerous other honors, including Italy's Rhegium Julii Prize and a National Endowment for the Arts fellowship. As a literary translator, De Robertis has rendered award-winning works by Laura Restrepo, Alejandro Zambra, Ray Loriga, Raquel Lubartowski Nogara, Roberto Ampuero, Marcos Aguinis, and Pedro Almodóvar, among others. In 2017, the Yerba Buena Center for the Arts named De Robertis on its 100 List of "people, organizations, and movements that are shaping the future of culture." She teaches at San Francisco State University and lives in Oakland, California, with her wife and two children.

KRISTIN DYKSTRA is principal translator of *The Winter Garden Photograph* by Cuban writer Reina María Rodríguez (Ugly Duckling Presse, 2019, with Nancy Gates Madsen), winner of the 2020 PEN Award for Poetry in Translation. She guest-edited "Out of Alamar," a dossier about poet Juan Carlos Flores (1962–2016) for the *Chicago Review* in 2018, and her translation of *Cubanology*, a multilingual book of days by Omar Pérez, appeared in the same year. Previously, she translated four books of contemporary Cuban poetry for the University of Alabama Press, including *The World as Presence* by Marcelo Morales, longlisted for the National Translation Award.

CLAYTON ESHLEMAN has translated a diverse array of voices throughout his influential career, including Antonin Artaud and Aimé Césaire. His forty-five years working on César Vallejo culminated in *The Complete Poetry: A Bilingual Edition* (2017). It was awarded the Academy of American Poets' Landon Translation Prize, two decades after Eshleman first won it for Vallejo's masterpiece, *Trilce* (1992). Eshleman also won the 1979 National Book Award for Translation for *The Complete Posthumous Poetry* of Vallejo. Author of numerous books of his own poetry, Eshleman also founded and edited the innovative journals *Caterpillar* and *Sulfur*. A combination of poetry and prose, his *Juniper Fuse: Upper Paleolithic Imagination & the Construction of the Underworld* charts Eshleman's long fascination with the prehistoric cave paintings of southwestern

France. It was published in 2003, the same year he was named emeritus professor of English at Eastern Michigan University.

GEORGE EVANS is a poet, political writer, and translator. A veteran of the Vietnam American War, his writings reflect his dedication as an antiwar activist, advocate for the homeless, and overall promoter of social change. The winner of fellowships from the California Arts Council, the Lannan Foundation, and the National Endowment for the Arts, he is the author of five books of poetry including *The New World* (Curbstone Press, 2002) and *Sudden Dreams* (Coffee House Press, 1991). He has also published two volumes of translations, both from Curbstone Press: *The Time Tree* (2003), by the Vietnamese poet Huu Thinh, and *The Violent Foam* (2002), by his wife, the Nicaraguan poet Daisy Zamora. They live in San Francisco.

CARL FISCHER is associate professor of Spanish and Latin American Studies in the Department of Modern Languages and Literatures at Fordham University; he also teaches in Fordham's Latin American and Latinx Studies Institute. Carl is the author of *Queering the Chilean Way: Cultures of Exceptionalism and Sexual Dissidence, 1965–2015* (Palgrave MacMillan, 2016) and the co-editor of *Chilean Cinema in the Twenty-First Century World* (Wayne State University Press, 2020). He has published scholarly articles on Latin American literature, gender studies, and film in journals such as *Hispanic Review, American Quarterly, Comunicación y medios*, and *Revista de Estudios Hispánicos*.

DAVID WILLIAM FOSTER was Regents' Professor of Spanish and Women and Gender Studies at Arizona State University, where he was head of the program in Spanish and Portuguese. His research focused on urban culture in Latin America, with special emphasis on Buenos Aires and São Paulo and on gender issues and Jewish diasporic culture. His most recent research focused on urban photography, and his book, *The City as Photographic Text: The Urban Photography of São Paulo*, is forthcoming with the University of Pittsburgh Press. Foster undertook numerous translations of Latin American literary works, including classics of Chicano literature originally written in Spanish.

KATHERINE M. HEDEEN is a translator, literary critic, and essayist. A specialist in Latin American poetry, she has translated some of the most respected voices from the region. Her publications include book-length collections by Jorgenrique Adoum, Juan Bañuelos, Juan Calzadilla, Juan Gelman, Fayad Jamís, Hugo Mujica, José Emilio Pacheco, Víctor Rodríguez Núñez, and Ida Vitale, among many others. She is a recipient of two NEA Translation Grants in the US, and a PEN Translates award in the UK. She is the associate editor for Action Books and the poetry in translation editor at the *Kenyon Review*. She resides in Ohio, where she is professor of Spanish at Kenyon College.

JUAN FELIPE HERRERA, the son of migrant farm workers, was named California's Poet Laureate in 2012 and served two terms as the United States Poet Laureate (2015–2017), the first Latino poet to receive this honor. He received an Educational Opportunity Program scholarship to attend UCLA, where he became active in the Chicano Civil Rights Movement. He later earned an MA in Social Anthropology from Stanford and an MFA from the University of Iowa Writers' Workshop. Herrera's numerous poetry collections include *187 Reasons Mexicanos Can't Cross the Border: Undocuments 1971–2007*, winner of the PEN West Poetry Award and the PEN Oakland National Literary Award for 2008, and *Notes on the Assemblage*, named a 2015 *New Yorker* Best Book of the Year (both volumes from City Lights Books). Passionate about writing for young people, Herrera has also published many books for children and middle-grade readers, such as his lauded work *Jabberwalking* (Candlewick, 2018), aimed at inspiring young poets.

JACK HIRSCHMAN is Poet Laureate emeritus of San Francisco. He has translated Dalton (Spanish), Depestre (French), Pasolini (Italian), Pastakas (Greek), Gervalla (Albanian), Kirsch (German), Glik (Yiddish), Laraque (Haitian), Mayakovsky (Russian), and Stalin (Georgian/Groozy). *The Arcanes*, Hirschman's thousand-page masterwork of his own verse, was published in 2006.

JOAN JARA is a British-born dancer, choreographer, and political activist. In the 1950s, touring Europe with the famed modern dance company Ballets Jooss, she married a fellow member, a Chilean. They moved to Santiago where she taught dance to theater students at the University of Chile. Her husband left her in 1960. In 1961, she met Víctor Jara, a student in the theater school. Víctor would become a legendary singer; Joan continued to teach. After Víctor was tortured and assassinated following the military's 1973 coup, Joan fled with their two daughters to England. She returned in 1983, the same year she published a memoir, *Víctor: An Unfinished Song*. She has fought tirelessly for human rights and for justice for her husband and other victims of the regime. In 1999, she received a dance award from the Municipality of Santiago. In 2009, the Chilean Senate awarded her Chilean nationality for her work to promote a return to democracy.

TOM JONES is a poet, translator, educator, and international human rights lawyer, an honors graduate of Harvard University (BA 1965), Columbia University School of Law (JD 1968), and George Mason University (MFA 1992), with undergraduate language and literature studies at the University of Paris-Sorbonne, the University of Madrid, the University of Munich, and the Goethe-Institut. Jones has published ten collections of poems, most recently *Nearing Palenque: Reflections on Native America* (FootHills Publishing, 2012) and *Beyond Existentialism* (FootHills, 2017), which features his poems with a selection of his black-and-white photographs. Jones has also published his translations of the late Spanish poet Miguel Hernandez's poems, *Songbook of Absences* (The Charioteer Press, 1972; reprinted 1980), and, with the author, Dominican poet Rei Berroa's Spanish poems, *Book of Fragments* (Writers Workshop, 1992). He was special guest writer at the sixteenth Rocky Mountain Writers Festival in Pocatello, Idaho, March 27–April 1 (2006).

AKIRA NISHIMURA was born in the state of Paraná, Brazil, and is currently living in the city of São Paulo with his partner Glauco Mattoso. He lived abroad for almost ten years, including four years in Japan as a dekassegui (someone of Japanese descent working abroad), and in Canada, where he earned a BA in General Studies from Redeemer University College. Nishimura then returned to Brazil to start his language teaching career. In

2009, he published his first book of short homoerotic stories, *The Apprentice*, with Black Devil Press. He is currently revising his partner's books while teaching classes at a language school.

IDRA NOVEY is a novelist, poet, and translator. She is the award-winning author of the novels *Those Who Knew* and *Ways to Disappear*. Her work has been translated into twelve languages, and she has translated numerous authors from Spanish and Portuguese, most recently Clarice Lispector. For her poetry and translation she has received awards from the PEN Translation Fund, the National Endowment for the Arts, and the Poetry Foundation. Her co-translations (with Ahmad Nadalizadeh) of Iranian poet Garous Abdolmalekian came out with Penguin in 2020.

WILLIAM O'DALY has translated eight books of Pablo Neruda's late-career and posthumous poetry, and most recently Neruda's first volume, *Book of Twilight*, a finalist for the 2018 Northern California Book Award in Translation. All were published by Copper Canyon Press. O'Daly's chapbooks of poems include *The Whale in the Web* (Copper Canyon), *The Road to Isla Negra* (Folded Word Press, 2015), *Water Ways* (Folded Word, 2017, a collaboration with JS Graustein), and *Yarrow and Smoke* (Folded Word's 2018 Masters Series title). A National Endowment for the Arts Fellow, O'Daly was a finalist for the 2006 Quill Award in Poetry and was profiled by Mike Leonard for *The Today Show*. O'Daly is a four-time Pushcart Prize nominee, and his essay "Creative Collisions: Poetry as a Transformative Act" was a finalist in *Tiferet Journal*'s 2018 Writing Contest.

BARBARA PASCHKE has been involved in translation for many years, as translator, editor, and advocate. She co-edited and was a contributing translator to two collections of Central American literature, *Volcán* (poetry) and *Clamor of Innocence* (short stories), and translated Daisy Zamora's *Riverbed of Memory* (all from City Lights Books). Paschke also edited Roque Dalton's *Clandestine Poems* (Curbstone). She has translated literary travel companions to Costa Rica, Cuba, and Spain. Her translations have appeared in numerous journals and anthologies, including writing on the Zapatista movement, *First World, Ha Ha Ha!* (City Lights Books), and *Tomorrow Triumphant*, selected poems of Otto René Castillo (Night Horn Books). She has served as board member and conference organizer for the American Literary Translators Association, for which she is also the initiator and host of the conference's annual Declamación. Paschke serves on the board of the Center for the Art of Translation.

JESSICA POWELL has published dozens of translations of literary works by a wide variety of Latin American writers. She was the recipient of a 2011 National Endowment for the Arts Translation Fellowship in support of her translation of Antonio Benítez Rojo's novel, *Woman in Battle Dress* (City Lights, 2015), a finalist for the PEN Center USA Literary Award for Translation. Her translation of *Wicked Weeds* by Pedro Cabiya (Mandel Vilar Press, 2016) was a finalist for the 2017 Best Translated Book Award and made the longlist for the 2017 National Translation Award. Other translations include Pablo Neruda's book-length poem, *venture of the infinite man* (City Lights Books, 2017); Adolfo Bioy Casares and Silvina Ocampo's *Where There's Love, There's Hate* (Melville House, 2013) and Silvina Ocampo's *The Promise* (City Lights Books, 2019) (both co-translated with Suzanne Jill Levine); Edna Iturralde's *Green Was My Forest* (Mandel Vilar Press, 2018); and Gabriela Wiener's *Nine Moons* (Restless Books, 2020).

VÍCTOR RODRÍGUEZ NÚÑEZ is one of Cuba's most outstanding and celebrated contemporary writers, with over fifty collections of poetry published throughout the world. He has been the recipient of major awards all over the Spanish-speaking region, including, in 2015, the coveted Loewe Prize. His selected poems have been translated into Arabic, Chinese, English, French, German, Hebrew, Italian, Macedonian, Serbian, and Swedish. He has been a riveting presence at the most important international literary festivals, having read in more than forty countries. In the last decade, his work has developed an enthusiastic readership in the US and the UK, where he has published seven book-length translations. He divides his time between Gambier, Ohio, where he is currently professor of Spanish at Kenyon College, and Havana, Cuba.

NORMAN SHAPIRO was a professor of Romance Languages and Literatures and distinguished professor of Literary Translation at Wesleyan University. Shapiro's translations of a vast array of French poetry, theater, and fiction have been widely published. His *Four Farces* by Georges Feydeau was nominated for a National Book Award, and *One Hundred and One Poems* by Paul Verlaine won the Modern Language Association of America's Scaglione Prize. Shapiro's scholarship on French Caribbean poetry and the Négritude movement has been influential. He conceived of, edited, and was one of the principal translators for

Négritude: Black Poetry from Africa and the Caribbean. First published in 1970, it is considered a fundamental anthology.

KATHERINE SILVER has translated more than forty works of contemporary and modern literature written in Spanish. Her most recent and forthcoming publications include works by María Sonia Cristoff, Daniel Sada, César Aira, Julio Cortázar, Juan Carlos Onetti, and Julio Ramón Ribeyro. She is the former director of the Banff International Literary Translation Centre (BILTC), and the author of *Echo Under Story* (What Books Press, 2019). She does volunteer legal interpreting for asylum seekers.

ANNETTE SMITH is a scholar and translator whose literary translations have focused primarily on Aimé Césaire, helping to bring about a revival of interest in the Martiniquais poet. Some of her most important translations include *Césaire: The Collected Poetry* (University of California Press, 1983), crafted in collaboration with Clayton Eshleman, hailed as a fundamental work for readers of twentieth-century poetry. She also worked with Eshleman on a translation of Césaire's masterful and highly influential long poem, *Notebook of a Return to the Native Land* (Wesleyan, 2001). In collaboration with Dominic Thomas, she published *Like a Misunderstood Salvation and Other Poems* (Northwestern University Press, 2013), containing poems from the beginning and end of Césaire's career, as well as previously deleted poems from *Solar Throat Slashed*. A scholar of nineteenth-century French literature, Smith began teaching at the California Institute of Technology in 1970. She has served as professor of literature emeritus since 1993.

EMILY TODER is a translator, poet, and archivist. She received degrees in literary translation from the University of East Anglia in Norwich, UK, and the Universitat Pompeu Fabra in Barcelona, Spain, and is a graduate of the MFA Program for Poets & Writers at the University of Massachusetts, Amherst. She has translated poetry, prose, and plays by Felipe Benítez Reyes, Laura Fernández, and Edgar Bayley, among other Spanish and Latin American writers, and is the author of several poetry collections and chapbooks. She lives in her native New York City where she runs a tiny letterpress operation and works in information management.

WILL VANDERHYDEN is a freelance translator, with an MA in Literary Translation from the University of Rochester. He has translated the work of Carlos Labbé, Rodrigo Fresán, and Fernanda García Lao, among others. Vanderhyden's translations have appeared in journals such as *Two Lines*, the *Literary Review*, the *Scofield*, and the *Arkansas International*. He has received fellowships from the NEA and the Lannan Foundation. His translation of *The Invented Part* by Rodrigo Fresán won the 2018 Best Translated Book Award.

PAUL M. WORLEY is an associate professor of global literature at Western Carolina University. He is the author of *Telling and Being Told: Storytelling and Cultural Control in Contemporary Yucatec Maya Literatures* (2013; with oral performance from this book project at www.tsikbalichmaya.org), and with Rita M. Palacios is co-author of *Unwriting Maya Literature: Ts'íib as Recorded Knowledge* (2019). He is a Fulbright Scholar and a 2018 winner of the Sturgis Leavitt Award from the

Southeastern Council on Latin American Studies. In addition to his academic work, Worley has translated selected works by Indigenous authors such as Hubert Malina, Adriana López, and Ruperta Bautista, and serves as editor-at-large for Mexico for the journal of world literature in English translation, *Asymptote*, as well as poetry editor for the *North Dakota Quarterly*.

RICHARD ZENITH was born in Washington, DC, but has lived for many years in Lisbon, where he works as a freelance writer, translator, researcher, and critic. He has published poems and short stories but is best known for his work on Fernando Pessoa. Besides preparing numerous editions, such as the *Livro do Desassossego* (which he later translated into English as *The Book of Disquiet*) and the seven-volume *Obra Essencial de Fernando Pessoa*, he has published essays on Pessoa and translated much of his poetry and prose into English. Zenith has also translated poetry by the Galician-Portuguese troubadours, Luís de Camões, Sophia de Mello Breyner, João Cabral de Melo Neto, Carlos Drummond de Andrade, and many living poets.

MARC ZIMMERMAN has helped lead LACASA, a publishing and resource center that looks at Latin American and Latino cultural studies through a globalization perspective, since he was named its first director in 1988. He now leads LACASA Chicago, specializing in Chicago Latino art and literature. Two of the many books he has written outside of LACASA include *Literature and Resistance in Guatemala* (Ohio University Press, 1995) and *Literature and Politics in the Central American Revolutions* (University of Texas Press, 1990). His translations of Central American poets have appeared in many journals. He is professor emeritus of Latin American and Latino Studies at the University of Illinois in Chicago, and of World Cultures and Literatures at the University of Houston, where he served as chair from 2002 to 2008. Zimmerman served on the jury of Casa de las Américas and has won Fulbright and Rockefeller Fellowships, among other major awards.

ACKNOWLEDGMENTS

The editors would like to thank the following people, among others, for their openhearted help in realizing this project: Naomi Ayala, Amy and Peter Bernstein, Abram Brosseit, Gilbert and Rona Eisner, Forrest Gander, María José Gutierrez, Claire Jaureguy, Gwen Kirkpatrick, Tania Lagos, Emma Lightizer, Courtney Maum, Catherine Murphy, Jacob Potts, Rodrigo Rojas, Vivaldo Santos, Pío E. Serrano, María Milagros Terán, Francisca Torres, and the librarians at the Library of Congress's Hispanic Division.

We were able to sustain our work over the length of this project because of inspiring individuals who have supported Red Poppy, the literary nonprofit behind this book.

We are very proud to have Tin House as our publisher. They put their own social action behind the words they print. Gratitude to the Publisher, Craig Popelars, and along with the entire team, we thank Jakob Vala for the book's stunning design work, and Nanci McCloskey and Molly Templeton for their magnificent marketing. We are so fortunate to have worked with Editorial Director Masie Cochran. Her belief in this project has moved us. She and fellow editors Elizabeth DeMeo and Alyssa Ogi quickly had a vision for the book that surpassed our own, and they implemented it, as if magically.

A thank you, in each of their languages, to the altruistic poets and translators who contributed their work with such trust and selflessness. We'd like to especially express our gratitude to Jessica Powell for her unstinting help with multiple aspects of the book; not only did she contribute several translations to the volume, she also employed her deft translation talent as an editor, which was particularly indispensable. Jessica's combination of intellectual and creative brilliance, along with inner warmth, is rare and so appreciated as a collaborator and as a friend.

Thank you to Julia Alvarez as well, for believing in this book and crafting such a compelling introduction.

And finally, to the memories of David William Foster and Michael Predmore, two beloved friends who have passed during the creation of this book. Their work on resistance both in and out of the classroom will continue to inspire for generations to come.

CREDITS